This May Sound Crazy

Abigail Breslin

HARPER

An Imprint of HarperCollinsPublishers

www.harpercollinschildrens.com

Library of Congress Control Number: 2015946374

ISBN 978-0-06-241482-3

Typography by Chelsea C. Donaldson

15 16 17 18 19 CG/RRDH 10 9 8 7 6 5 4 3 2 1

❖

First Edition

The events and experiences detailed herein are true and have been faithfully rendered as remembered by the author, to the best of her abilities. Some names and identifying characteristics have been changed to protect the privacy and anonymity of the individuals involved.

Why I'm Writing This

Ever since I was really little, I loved writing. I just liked telling stories. When I was twelve, I wrote a short story for the first time. It was about a girl in a mental institution with schizophrenia. My parents were terribly concerned. I'm sure they hoped I just had a "big imagination."

But that first story opened something up for me; writing became like my friend. A person I can say whatever I feel to.

Then in 2013, when I was really into poetry, my friend told me to look at a certain Tumblr page. Almost immediately I was hooked. After hours of scrolling through photos of sunsets and cobblestone streets and different quotes and stories, I felt like I knew the people who had created them. I knew what

they liked and disliked—from bands to foods to movies to whether or not they got along with their parents to who they had a crush on. Tumblr quickly became a place where I could tell stories about guys I liked who didn't like me back or friends who gave me advice that I wanted to share. I began messaging back to the people who followed my blogs, and they shared stories with me about their exes and their friends, about their recent heartbreaks and their newfound loves—and sometimes just about their cats or their dog. They would just ask me things like "You know when you text someone something really long and they send back one-word answers? What's up with that?" . . . Like, girl, I FEEL YOU.

Writing on Tumblr was a way for me to feel like I wasn't alone. Other people were going through the same things I was, feeling the same feels I did.

Because yes, I haven't had the most typical of lives. I've been making movies since I was five years old. And I'm sure some people reading this are thinking "She has no idea what it's like to see the guy who just broke up with you at school every day!" and those people would be right. I don't. I was homeschooled my entire life, but not necessarily because of acting. I have two older brothers, Ryan and Spencer. Ryan is in his thirties, and he was also homeschooled by my parents. Ryan was never an actor; it was just a choice my parents made. Once my brother Spencer started acting, though, the whole homeschooling thing worked out really well. People always ask if I felt isolated or not socialized. But, to be honest, the only thing more dramatic than teen drama, is teen ACTOR drama. All of the emotions, with the most dramatized reactions.

No, I don't know what it's like to see the guy

who dumped you at school every day. BUT, I know what it's like to see the guy who dumped you on TV every day. Or on set every day. Or at events where reporters are talking to him and telling him how brilliant he is and then—BLAM!—he also books the biggest movie in the world and then you just know you're gonna see him even MORE than all the time and how is there possibly any more time than all the time and—

Okay. Sorry . . . Ranting.

The point is, just because I haven't had the same life as a lot of people, I have the same feelings. Just different settings. And so because not everyone in the world uses Tumblr, I thought I'd write this. To be real. To share. So that maybe I can help one person text their ex the appropriate emoji. (Always the squinted-eye, "you ain't foolin' me, honey" one. Just always.)

This IS what matters, folks.

Enjoy

Table of

Contents

1

REASONS
TO NOT
STALK
YOUR EX

We've all done it, guys.
No judgment here.

It's late. You're tired. You know it's wrong, but you still find yourself looking through your ex's Instagram posts. Who liked it? Who commented on it? Is he with a girl?!

The anxiety never ends. I've made the mistake countless times. Stalking your ex is NEVER a good idea.

Here Are Reasons Why NOT TO STALK YOUR S.O.'s EX.

1 I believe it was Teddy Roosevelt who said, "Comparison is the thief of joy." (Teddy clearly knew heartbreak, imo!) I know we all tend to worry/wonder about the obvious questions: "Is she prettier than me?" "Is she skinnier/curvier than me?" "Does she have bigger boobs than me?" "Was she better in ~sexy situations~ than me?" Tbh, guys don't really think about that. They honestly don't compare. It just doesn't happen; it just doesn't work that way. Trust me.

2 THEY BROKE UP FOR A REASON. Okay, this is one that's a little more complicated than "it wasn't meant to be," and I get that. Sometimes maybe he'll tell you, "I broke up with her," but then you've heard stories that she broke up with him. Or maybe they've had one of those ~annoying~ on-and-off things where they kept breaking up and getting back together over and over again, and your fear is that it all might happen again. So let me save you a little bit of heartache on this—if you think there's a possibility they're gonna get right back together: STOP NOW. At the end of the day, you never know for sure what's gonna happen, but if you have a suspicion this is just another one of their off periods, tell him to call you when he knows what he wants. Or maybe he was just with his ex for a long time, and it makes you feel kinda small in his life. That's normal, too. They have all these memories and stories together that you don't have yet. But ultimately, you're going to make your own memories and stories with them. Every relationship has its ups and downs, BUT they aren't together anymore. And sometimes, no matter how hard it may be, we just have to accept that and trust the person we are with is with US for a reason.

3 Stalking your bae's ex on social media won't make her relationship with your S.O. disappear. They dated. IT HAPPENED. You have exes, too. Think about it this way, when you're with your current ~lover~ do you always think about your ex? NO! You don't. Instead you worry about THEIR exes. Don't you think maybe your S.O. feels the same? And if you ARE thinking about your ex, you might have a bigger problem, like, why are you with this new bae at all?

And finally: You're worth more than that. You are worthy of being with and being loved and adored. Stressing about your S.O.'s past relationship is crazy. It's in the past. You can't change it. You can't make it go away. History is history. Your only choice is to move on with your life. Realize the person you are with now is with you because they WANT to be WITH YOU. Stressing about past things only adds worry and insecurity, which just isn't ever romantic.

And Now for Reasons to Not Stalk YOUR Ex:

Why did you guys break up? Repeat your breakup convo in your head when you feel like checking his/her news feed. If you were the one to end things, you made the right decision. It may take a while to be okay with it, but you had a reason to do something that couldn't have been fun or easy. Remember that. And if THEY were the one to end things, they were dumb for leaving you. I know I don't know you—but it's the truth. It's their loss. They just don't know it yet. And if neither works, if you still are feeling heart-heavy and super sad, then you probably need to talk to them, face-to-face, to get closure before you move on.

2 It's just one person! This is easier said than done—BELIEVE me, I know. I have been known to be bedridden over break-ups. (It happens.) But at the end of the day, I remind myself that there are more than seven billion people in the world and it's crAzy to let any ONE person dictate my life. Especially one I'm not with anymore.

3 You can't control them. If they choose to be with someone else, then . . . that sucks. It will hurt. You will ugly cry and most likely send them a billion texts that are incoherent, and you will show up at your best friend's apartment sobbing and begging for cuddles. (Not that this has happened to me or anything . . . ha!) But at the end of the day you can't control them. You have to accept there is a reason you aren't with them anymore. It takes time, but you'll come to peace with it. Trust me, you will.

4 You are worth more. You will move on and you will be okay. You might not feel it RIGHT now, but I promise you it's true. Life isn't always fair, but love is. Even when you think it's not. You will realize that there are people out there who will want to be with you and treat you right. And hopefully, one day, you can call your ex and have a nice conversation about your new partners. It CAN happen. It DOES happen. Hang on. Hold tight. I promise you'll survive.

But until then, if you really can't handle seeing their posts . . . Block them. Yes, it seems like an act of war, but your mental health and sanity come first. The only way to not check up on them is to not have the option to. I promise you it will feel SO liberating. They might be pissed, sure. But in time they will understand, and a possible friendship will be more likely if you both have the space and time to rehab your emotions.

At the end of the day, the best thing to do is go to a local park (I am #blessed to call my local park Central Park), turn your phone on Airplane mode (so U don't receive any texts or notifications), and listen to your favorite playlist. I do that before I send any angry texts or look at my ex's profile. At the end of my walk, I've usually calmed down and realized that it's just not worth it.

Then again, sometimes . . .

Well, I'm just curious who that girl is who
liked his profile picture on September 8,
and now I'm on her cousin's husband's best
friend's page . . .

He's kinda cute. UGH.

MY

CHRISTMAS

OBSESSION

It's 2:53 a.m. I'm in bed in Christmas paja-mas*, watching *The Family Stone***, and did I mention it's June?

> ME: Hi, my name is Abbie, and I have a Christmas addiction.
>
> YOU: Hi, Abbie.

I don't really know exactly when my obses-sion with Christmas happened. I'd like to think I was just born this way (cue Lady Gaga; love you, gurl), because I've always had this strange affinity for all things Christmas. It started full force when I was fourteen. My brothers, Ryan and Spencer, had both moved out, and I had become the only child. I was used to Ryan being gone

*actually serious
**also actually serious

because he's eleven years older than me, and he went to college in Washington, DC, when I was really young. He'd come back for the summer and stay with us. But when I say "stay with us," I mean he'd eat with us and shower and then go out with his friends. TEENAGERS, AMIRITE?

But Spencer is only four years older than me. He'd always been in the next room playing his guitar LOUDLY (which was super annoying because I was TRYING to listen to the *High School Musical* sound track on repeat UNDISTURBED). And although he was (and still is) an annoying big brother, I guess it was comforting having him there. Like, when I got in trouble with my parents, he understood what it was like.

But as I said: They're both still annoying cuz they will read this and think I think they're cool.

WHICH
CAN
HAP
O

And for a while after Spencer left it was cool on my own cuz I could just do whatever I wanted. I could play guitar and talk on the phone loudly about *Glee* without my brothers bothering me. But then I got kinda lonely. The apartment felt quiet and empty. I started to take a lot of comfort in knowing that they'd be home for Thanksgiving and Christmas. I looked forward to it.

So . . .

I started watching Christmas movies. All the time. And listening to Christmas music. ALL THE TIME. IT WAS INSANITY.

I actually got yelled at for blasting Christmas music in my room late one night.

And it got to the point that whenever I was sad, I put on something like *The Family Stone* or *Christmas with the Kranks* or *A Christmas Carol* (the one with George C. Scott) or *Elf* or one of the other million Christmas movies I love, and I felt better.

A lot better.

I guess for me, Christmas is the one time of year when everything is COMPLETELY okay. And I mean usually things are okay, but this is when it's FULLY okay. Like no boy drama or friend drama cuz everyone is just too happy eating gingerbread and chillin' to be worried. . . . Okay, LAST year I had boy drama, but I mean IRRELEVANT. My whole family, some friends, my dogs and cats (and my turtle) are there. Everyone is there at Christmas . . . and everything just feels good and comfortable.

The point is . . .

Yes, it's a strange obsession. Usually people are just like, "Oh my God, it's so cold out, can't wait for summer." But I think summer is gross. Like, no offense, summer, but you are hot and humid and you mess up my eyeliner. And you make me tired. COLD AIR MAKES YOU FEEL EXCITED FOR HOLIDAY FESTIVITIES. No? Just me?

Well, okay, sometimes I wish winter would end like . . . January 2. . . . But . . . Yeah . . . Can't always get what you want, I guess.

¯_(ツ)_/¯

But, I think if there's one thing that you can always turn toward to make you feel better, even for a moment, you should hold on to that. Some people don't have something like that. So if you do, whether it is Christmas or something else, who cares if it's cheesy?

(And since when do people dislike cheese so much? I like cheese. I think cheese is a great food. Especially mozzarella, which we buy from Russo's in NYC on Christmas Eve and it's AMAZING.)

Okay, sorry. This is not a cheese chapter, though now I might make one cuz I really think cheese is underrated as a food group. Is it a food group? No. But dairy is. And what is in cheese? DAIRY.

I thought I'd add my Christmas routine so that you'd get a feel for why it's so strange that I'm so obsessed with the holiday season.

🕐 9:00 a.m.

I wake up, go into the living room to see my family for a split second before I beeline to my stocking.

🕙 10:00 a.m.

I drag myself off of the couch and head out with my family to go to church.

🕥 10:10 a.m.

We stop at Starbucks on the way cuz I'm cliché. I also get a peppermint hot chocolate OR eggnog latte cuz again #BASICBITCH.

🕚 11:00 a.m.

We get to church. We church it up. 🙌 #praise

① 12:30 p.m.

I stop at Bagels on the Square off Bleecker Street and pick up a bunch of bagels and some different cream cheese spreads. My favorite is a cinnamon-raisin bagel, toasted, with Dutch apple cream cheese cuz YOLO. My brothers go get Ess-a-Bagel for everyone else. It's a family rivalry that will never be settled. #bagellove

① 1:30 p.m.

I am now back in my pajamas and eating and my family has started opening presents.

⊖ 2:45 p.m.

It's that awkward moment when someone gives you a gift and you don't understand why their brain thought it would be a good idea to give you said gift, so you're just like "Omg thank you so kind of you thx," but in your head, your inner monologue is like "Bitch, please."

🕐 5:00 p.m.

Gift opening is coming to an end. WE HAVE A LARGE FAMILY. WE ARE NOT WASTE-FUL, OKAY?

🕐 8:00 p.m.

After everyone has taken a slothlike nap from all the Christmas treats, we all go out to dinner at Tony's. We are super orig.

🕐 10:30 p.m.

We come home, watch a movie (*The Grinch*), and go to sleep cuz we are all tuckered out from all of our festiveness.

z z Sleep.
z   z   z   z   z

Anyway. Now that you've LITERALLY gotten a play-by-play of my entire EXISTENCE, I hope this recipe for my great-great-grandmother's nutmeg cookies makes it better.

NUTMEG COOKIES

(AKA THE MOST DELICIOUS THINGS YOU WILL EVER EAT IN YOUR ENTIRE LIFE. THEY ARE JUST FILLED WITH WINTER JOY AND THEY WILL WARM YOUR SOUL TO ITS VERY CORE.)

1 cup sugar

½ cup shortening

¼ tsp. salt

½ tsp. nutmeg

2 eggs

1 cup buttermilk

½ tbsp. baking soda

2 cups flour

Mix it all together in a big bowl.

Roll it into little two-inch-wide cookie balls.

Grease a cookie sheet.

Throw it in the oven, 15 minutes, pre-heated to 350 degrees.

3

WONDER-
LAND

Picture this: Me in the middle of an Italian restaurant at the Grove, an outdoor shopping center in LA. I'm getting a call from my doctor to tell me my allergic reaction was actually "Coxsackievirus." To which I replied, "But doctor! I don't even have a boyfriend!

[I'M DISGUSTING.]

ANYWAY . . . This particular virus is most commonly seen in little kids who eat glue :) For me, I got it on an airplane. It causes hives on your feet, hands, and scalp. Not very cute—and itchy as HELL.

As I sat in the restaurant, Summer* walked in. Summer was (and is again) one of my best friends. I met her on Twitter, of course, through a bunch of mutual friends, who told us we had a TON in common. For example, we freaked out about guys and makeup the same way. Summer was super fun. Back then she had this really long mermaid hair that was naturally brown but she always longed to dye it blonde. And she had this way of making everywhere she went seem cooler and everyone she was with feel more important.

Before I even sat down to join the table, Summer started explaining to me that she had decided to move to London. She had met Joel* there in November and she really liked him. They had discussed her moving there, but I never believed it would happen till now. Now it felt suddenly real.

Honestly, I was scared.

The person who had gotten me through the past four months was leaving the country. How would I survive the bad days (especially the bad eyeliner days)?! The last year had been tough. I had been obsessed with two different guys and both crushes ended HORRIBLY. Literally, one guy was just your average, everyday jerk. I was apparently the "only girl" he was seeing, but alas! WASN'T.

Shocking, I know. The other guy was one I actually really cared about. He was a good friend of mine before we started dating, and we ended up in one of those awful Non-relationship Relationships (refer to Chapter 16: "The Dangers of Non-relationship Relationships").

But Summer was always there for me. She was the only friend I could TRULY count on for vent sessions over Skype and a constant stream of hilarious yet uplifting texts. TWIN FLAMES. And now she was leaving the COUNTRY? What was I honestly gonna do?

But she was happy and I was happy for her and I didn't want her to think otherwise SO . . .

I told her to find me a British boyfriend. Duh.

She told me about this guy Matt*, who was her boyfriend Joel's friend. She had never met him but heard Joel talking about him a lot. So I did what I do and followed Matt on Twitter, but he never DM'ed me. (No hard feelings, Matt!) He probably didn't DM me because HE DIDN'T KNOW ME. (THANKS, SUMMER, for making me look insane. ☺)

After lunch was over and Summer left, I realized how sad I was. I mean, my best friend had decided to move to another country! We promised to Skype and text all the time, but still . . .

We Skyped as soon as she got to London. I remember she was blow-drying her hair on the floor of Joel's room. They were about to go meet Adam* at the pub. "The pub" was always the meet-up spot for them, but it isn't a specific place. It kinda just means a lot of different restaurant/bars. The legal drinking age in the UK is eighteen btw, and Summer was nineteen. (I was still seventeen . . . but hey, R-rated movies holllllllaaaaaa.)

Needless to say, I was jealous of Summer by this point. (And yes, I know, she's only just arrived!) But she had everything I wanted. A cool boyfriend, independence, and happiness.

When I told Summer she had to find me a cool British boyfriend, one who'd get it when I was stalking them, Joel got an idea. He texted me the next morning saying that he found me a British boyfriend. SAY WHAAAAt.

I was obviously super skeptical cuz these kinds of setups never work out, right?

Right?
Like ever

After seeing his pic I was like 😍 🙌. Long story short, it was his friend Adam, the guy from the pub. We started talking and it turned out we had a lot in common. Adam was really nice and funny and cute and totally interesting and cool. You know when you first start liking someone and everything they say is like "Omg you're so poetic and wise." This was that. It was crazy how immediate it all was. We instantly started talking every single day. And Adam even asked me to be his valentine. I thought this was sweet but impossible, seeing how he was in London and I was in NYC. But he said we could have a Skype coffee date.

I kicked my family out of the surrounding rooms and spent the next hour adjusting my light dimmer (yes, I have a light dimmer; they are brilliant!) and fixing my makeup and choosing what to wear.

I prepared first with a group text with Summer and Joel, who coached me by saying things like:

SUMMER:

k abba remember not to show him your creepy weird doll head collection right away.

JOEL:

Ya, that's serious, abigail.

SUMMER:

don't have skype sex right away

ME:

SUMMER OMG THAT'S DISGUSTING. I HAVE TO GO. BYE HATERZ

SUMMER:

I love you

JOEL:

Love you both

THEN. THE SKYPE HAPPENED. It was weirdly awkward cuz the connection was bad. On SKYPE, I mean. On SKYPE, THE CONNECTION WAS BAD. THE LOVE CONNECTION . . . THAT WAS STRONG. Like, he was really cute and really funny and really smart and cool and—ughhhhhh—perfect, I guess.

After that, we were basically inseparable via Skype and text. We would have "double dates" on Skype with Summer and Joel. It really felt like things were going perfectly. The only thing was, I wondered how long we could keep this up with me being all the way in New York and him being in London. I knew I had to see him. But how . . .

This is where we delve into —

ABBIE'S BRILLIANT SCHEMES OF MANIPULATION.

I asked my mom, "Um, so Summer's really sad and lonely in London. Do you think I could go visit her for my birthday?"

My mom's initial reactions were a series of very cliché Mom questions such as:

"Is this for that boy?"
       "I don't think so."
               "London is very far away."
       "For how long?"
"How are you gonna finish your book?"

To which I was like:

"MOMMMMMMMMMMMM, I DON'T EVEN HAVE A PUBLISHER YET. THE BOOK IS JUST AN IDEA. IT'S AN EGG WITHOUT SPERM."

And then my mom said no and went to go get her nails done. (Note to self: Never fight with Mom about seeing a boyfriend by making egg-sperm arguments.)

Summer volunteered to text my mom and beg? But nah. My mom wouldn't go for that.

Luckily for me, my mom is totally a cool mom. When she got back she said, "If you can convince your dad, you can go."

YASSSSSS.

I knew this would be easy because if there's one thing I know my dad can't resist, it's tears.

Flash forward to me telling my dad, through sobs, that I really missed Summer and she was super homesick. After a lot of back and forth, he finally said yes.

So I booked my flight for April 10, 2014.

My mom, my brother Spencer, and his best friend, Trevor, came with me. My mom spent time with them while I went off with Summer, Joel, and Adam.

From the moment I got there, I knew London was where I belonged. I loved the city. I went to dinner with Summer the first night there and then met with Joel and Adam right after. These were the people I wanted to be with.

Summer and Joel ran into a frozen yogurt shop and told Adam and me to wait outside. I was, like, whaaa . . . until I realized why. Twenty seconds later, Adam kissed me. It wasn't so much that there were "fireworks" or whatever. More like I was hit by a train. Cupid laid me out, big-time.

The four of us spent the rest of the evening wandering the city before stopping to get tea. Because as stated previously, I was still only seventeen, which is still NOT the legal drinking age in London. So, my after-dinner drink was peppermint tea. The rest of my time there was spent walking through London, taking endless amounts of pictures and sharing secrets with the three of them that I have never shared with anyone else. Summer and I refer to this time as Wonderland. It was only two weeks of all four of us being there, but it felt like the world had slowed down and we had been together there for years.

We had fallen down the rabbit hole and landed on our heads and everything was upside down in the best way. I was so in love and in awe of these people. It all seemed so ideal and beautiful; I thought I was dreaming for most of it.

But I wasn't.
It was real.
IT HAPPENED.

For my eighteenth birthday, they took me to a club.

We spent most of the night being the lamest people in the club sitting at the table, drinking champagne (totally legal now in London!) and talking about our feelings. Lame? Maybe. But to us it was perfect.

Adam got up to use the restroom and Summer went to get another drink. Joel slid over next to me, put his arm around me, and whisper-shouted over "Talk Dirty to Me" (such a sentimental romantic song):

" We are gonna remember this for the rest of our lives. "

It sounds cheesy, but it was true.

That night was still, in my opinion, the best

time of my life so far.

Yes. So far.

I look back on it wishing I could go back there, knowing how awesome it was. But I think what made it so good was that I didn't see it coming.

I miss it. I miss that time. Not just the weeks I was there with all of them, but the weeks leading up to it and the weeks after. The whole five months when we were the most important people in each other's lives. I mean, think about how crazy it was: My best friend up and moves her life to London, falls madly in love with a British boy, introduces me to the British boy's best friend, WE fall in love, I randomly go to London for weeks to be with them, we have the most amazing time of our lives, and then just as quickly as it all began, it all ended. Summer flew back to the

States the same day I left London. I still don't know exactly why Summer left when she did. I know she says now it's just because she was sad, but I wish I had known then what made her leave. She and Joel planned to stay together, but they wound up breaking up a month later. And what it all showed me was that everything that happened was because of the four of us. Specifically us. You couldn't re-create that time with other people. One missing piece, and the whole thing comes crashing down.

So I know how hard it can be to let go of the past and move on when you don't feel like you'll ever have something that amazing again. But as Summer said to me today, "You were Alice and that was your Wonderland. But Alice had many stories. You just need to find a new Wonderland."

So I will.

I will.

4

HOW TO BE FRIENDS WITH BOTH PEOPLE IN A BREAKUP

Let me set up a visual for you.

I've just gotten back home from a "lunch." Like, one of those actual lunches that came about because someone said, "Let's do lunch." Like, that's a thing . . . Like, that actually happens.

ANYWAY . . .

I came home, immediately got into my pajamas (my brother says I hold the world record for quickest changer into pajamas), and checked my phone. Ten text messages from my friend Summer.

I'm busy piecing together bits of broken, incoherent text messages that looked something like this:

JOEL:

OGM LITERALLY I CANT EEVEN RIGHTR
NOW LIKE WTF

SUMMER:

Im so sad now i literally just like I'm dying

SUMMER:

whatevering over it ill find someone else

JOEL:

PLEASE ANSWER YOUR *expletive*
PHONE NOW.

Long before I got to the last message, I realized Joel was now Summer's *ex*-boyfriend.

But before I can call Summer back, Joel calls me about not wanting to break up with Summer.

Trying to be friends with both people in a breakup, I have learned, is near impossible. You're torn between taking two completely different sides usually, which isn't fair, and you can't help feeling like you're being a bad friend if you don't agree with both of them.

This makes things really, really, really, REALLLLLLY complicated. Especially when one person decides to tell the other person what you've been saying. THEN you're the person to blame. You can't win. And with Summer and Joel, I couldn't ever win.

Once they were in the throes of the breakup, Joel and Summer started arguing through me. . . . I mean there was even a time when

Summer had asked me to tell Joel that she'd just gotten her period. I guess so he knew she was in an extra bad mood so not to mess with her. . . . Which I was like, *Yeah, I feel you, girl.*

Periods suck.

But then when I told Joel, he was like, "I don't care. That's cool, but I don't care. Whatever."

And then just hung up and I was kinda like, "Bae, chill. I'm just the messenger here."

And also saying you don't care is VERY offensive cuz you're a dude. You don't know how hard it is to stay positive about life when you are literally the human form of the blood elevators in *The Shining*, okay?

Or there was the time when he asked me to ask Summer if she wanted him to send her back her pajamas.

And she texted me all like, "OH MY GOD, WHY ARE YOU STILL TALKING TO HIM? NO, I DON'T WANT MY PAJAMAS BACK. I'M NOT POOR. I CAN AFFORD NEW PAJAMAS. I HAVE PLENTY. I DONT NEED HIM SENDING ANYTHING TO ME AT ALL, EVER—NOT EVEN A GIFT. AND MY OLD PAJAMAS ARE DEFINITELY NOT A GIFT."

And I was like, "Okay."

And then he texted me and said, "WHAT DID SHE SAY? DOES SHE WANT HER PAJAMAS OR NOT? I HAVE A LIFE TO LIVE, AND I DONT HAVE TIME TO WAIT AROUND TO SEE IF SHE WANTS HER PAJAMAS. SO DOES SHE WANT THEM OR NOT? I HAVE THINGS TO DO, I HAVE PLANS AND THINGS I WANNA DO, AND PLACES I HAVE TO BE, AND FRIENDS I HAVE TO SEE AND THINGS. THINGS I NEED TO DO. SO DOES SHE WANT THEM?"

And I was like, "No."

And then for some reason they both HATED me after that.

For a while, at least. Then they both came back to me being all nice. I guess cuz they realized how fabulous I am and how hard it is to stay away from my amazingness. 💁

The moral of the story is: No good deed goes unpunished.

Now I'm not saying you shouldn't be there for both people if you're friends with the two of them. But trying to help them get back together will never work. Someone will always feel betrayed, no matter what your intent was.

And also, breakups happen for a reason! Someone—and usually both of them just don't realize it right away—is unhappy in the relationship. Trying to pressure them into going back to something that made them unhappy isn't fair. It can add a lot of stress to what's already incredibly stressful.

After both Summer and Joel started freaking out on me for talking to their ex

(which is each other.
Mind blown.
Sorry if this is confusing,)

I decided the best thing to do was to stay out of it. Trying to push two people together when they already are broken up never works out well—for anyone. Instead, I just told them that they have to work out their issues and that I would be there for both of them for emotional support/sad music recommendations/uplifting quotes I find on

Tumblr/*Dance Moms* trivia/adorable cat memes/Cards Against Humanity games. It didn't work out because one lived in London and one lived in LA, but still, I did my best.

I kinda felt like Dr. Phil.

And in the end, it actually wound up okay.

BTW, have I ever mentioned how much I ship Dr. Phil and his wife? But that's another story for another time. . . .

</3

Crystal Castles
(A She Poem)

To be with him always was all that she wanted
Her head on his chest
Their hands interlocking

To breathe in his air
Like a drag from a smoke
To give all she had
But all she had broke

See, her heart was too fragile
Encompassed by glass
Her own crystal castle
Too gorgeous to last

But still she had hope one day it would change
'cause later she learned
He too was the same

So together they built
From the rubble of guilt
Their own crystal castle
On top of a hill

A hill of secrets and all their regrets
The things he had promised
The things she forgets

And maybe together their hearts were less fragile
But easy to break
Inside crystal castles

It's been said before
That love shouldn't hurt
But here's my opinion
For what it is worth

Love isn't something that you could define
Not in a song
Or a book
Or even this line

Love is just something we feel when we know
It hurts less together
Than when we're alone

Yes, it does hurt
But all I'll say is this
I'd give 10 million hurts
Than one less of his kiss

'Cause here's my opinion
For all that it's worth
If I had a choice
In who'd break my heart
I'd rather him hurt me
Than all others by far

So together they built
From the rubble of guilt
Their own crystal castle
On top of a hill
A hill full of joy and nostalgic air
If it hurt to let go
It just meant they cared

Yes, maybe their hearts were less fragile
But easier to break
Inside crystal castles.

THE

TEN-TO-ONE

RULE

There is nothing in this world more terrifying than this.

You're by your phone, wondering why you haven't heard from you know who. BAE.

Well, maybe he's not bae yet, but you're hoping to make him bae.

Here's the thing:
boys are confusing.

They do things like text you like every day at, say, 1:00 p.m. for a week and then all of a sudden: *Nah, just not gonna text her today even though the last thing I texted her was* "Talk to U tomorrow."

And then you go crazy. You're all like: *Did that mean YOU'LL text ME tomorrow or that I should text YOU?* See, it's unclear, and now if I wait for you to text me you might not because you want me to text you and then we might not talk today and then it's not long before I'm thinking, *Wow, he really hates me. I should've texted him. I need to grow up and stop playing games.*

But then if I do send that text, all day I'm gonna be thinking, *He's only talking to me cuz he feels bad for me. He doesn't actually like me. What a GRAVE mistake I have made.*

So yeah. Boys are confusing and they suck.

Which is why, my dear friends, I am here to help you.

I have a friend named Nick Simmons and he is my official Boy Consultant. He's my friend Sophie's brother, and while she also gives ~bomb~ advice, sometimes it helps to hear a boy's perspective on the complicated and terrifying realm that is the male brain.

After texting Nick one night in a bit of a mild freak out that looked something like this:

Me: ····

NEED HELP RITE NOW

···· **Nick:**

Shoot.

Me: ····

OK SO LJKE WE HAVE BEEN TALKJNG NONSSTOP, BUT TODAY HE HASNT TDXTED ME YET. AND IDK. ITS LJKE WHY RNT U TEXTING ME? WHO R U WITH RIFHF NOW?! SHOULD I TEXT HIM OR NAH

See? Mild freak out.

Nick then proceeded to give me some of the best advice I have ever gotten. I refer to it as the Ten-to-One Rule. It's very simple yet VERY hard to follow.

But first let me start this by saying that we are all badass ~queens~ and we can text a guy WHENEVER we want and shouldn't feel bad about it at all. If you WANT to text a guy first, you SHOULD. It's 2015; we don't have to adhere to dumb clichés. However, from talking to Nick I've learned that a lot of guys, not all but a lot, really like the chase. Weird and dumb but true. So, if already you're like "NOPE, I'm gonna text him whenever I want idgaf" then you are way stronger than me, TEACH ME YOUR WAYS. If not, continue reading.

If a guy starts a text conversation with you five to eight days in a row, then you may start the conversation first ONCE. Got it? Five to eight days of him first means you get ONE day to text him first. It shows you are enjoying talking to him, too, but by then one text shouldn't scare him off. Then let him start the conversation five to eight days in a row again before you text him first again. I call it the Ten-to-One Rule cuz that's the ideal: To get him to text first ten times before you text him the one time—and so on and so forth until, of course, you're both in love. Then you can start texting him whenever.

ANYWAY, WAITING IS HARD. REALLY HARD. So for those days when you have already used up your one day of texting first, I have OTHER STRATEGIES.

My personal favorite is to have what I call a Stock Image System. On days when my hair looks good or I really like my outfit or my makeup—days where I don't look THAT different just especially saucy. 😏 I take advantage of that and take as many selfies in as many locations as possible. And then I save them so that I can post them on Instagram and Twitter and Facebook while he's online. A lot of time, it WORKS. He'll either comment or like it or outright text to say hi. Yeah. Boys suck. Like REALLY, GUYS, I HAD TO POST A GOOD SELFIE FOR YOU TO REMEMBER MY EXISTENCE?

But Nick says, "Maybe he just saw that as a

good excuse to text you."

Which is true.

Sometimes guys get nervous, too. WE ARE
ALL HUMAN.

The thing is to remember not to use too
many excuses, i.e.:

"Omg I just accidentally saw a tweet of yours
from 3 weeks ago where U said u like Breaking Bad. I'm at Barnes & Noble right now.
Should I get the first season? I've never seen
it."

$$\left\{ \text{Yes, this is something I have done.} \right\}$$

(And no, he didn't text back.)

And if any guy says they are just "bad at texting" . . . Well . . . What that usually means to me is "I'm bad at texting because I hate U."

Yeah, maybe that's dramatic, but I don't really get that whole excuse. A text takes thirty seconds to send. And if a guy wants to talk to you he WILL find the time to talk to you. Period.

And this is just a way to take out some of that anxiety over "Should I?/Shouldn't I?"

If nothing else, just read this chapter when you are about to make a rash decision. By the time you finish this, if you still want to text him DO IT.

We will get through these treacherous times together, kids.

Godspeed.

Godspeed

*Special thanks to Nick Simmons for being the best Boy Consultant and giving me this wonderful tip that has helped me through the most trying of times

A REAL-LIFE HALLOWEEN HORROR STORY

I love autumn. I love the look of fall leaves, the crisp air, pumpkin spice lattes. I long for those fall days when I can take a walk through the park. Yes, I am one of those ridiculously lucky people who calls Central Park my park. With an extra hot PSL in hand, a light jacket on, and a good playlist in my pocket, there's no place I'd rather be.

Does this make me sound like a sixty-five-year-old woman?
DON'T CARE.

ANYWAY . . . I love the fall. I am a fall enthusiast. I love going to the farmers' market in Union Square and getting apples. I love long drives with my mom and my brother Ryan and his girlfriend, April, to get pumpkins in New Jersey. And I love coming home, getting into pj's, and settling in to watch horror movies.

BECAUSE, YES, I ALSO LOVE HORROR

MOVIES. Horror is quite possibly my favorite genre.

In bed.

At home.

With my cats, dogs, and family surrounding me.

HOWEVER. Halloween itself?

WELL . . . not so much.

One year, my friends and I decided to go to Knott's Scary Farm. It was a trip that ended with me curled up into a ball on the ground sobbing because of the clowns being there . . . (IN FRONT OF MY CRUSH no less. NICELY DONE, ABIGAIL.)

Another Halloween, when I was around seven, ended after I rang someone's doorbell and what I thought was a FAKE plastic mummy turned out to be their son dressed up as a mummy. What did I do when it moved, you ask?

I threw all of my hard-earned candy on their lawn and ran SCREAMING and SOBBING down the hill to my parents' car.

YES.

My mom then made my brother, Spencer, go back to pick up all my candy.

THANKS, MOM. THANKS, SPENCER.

But there was one particular year that was even more horrifying than the rest.

Because, as you might learn throughout this book, there is no horror film, no haunted house, no Halloween parlor trick in the world that is quite as horrifying as the inside of a fifteen-year-old girl's mind.

So let us flash back to Halloween 2011. . . .

Let me preface by saying that I have NEVER been cool. And that isn't some self-deprecating "I hate myself" statement. I like myself plenty. I just have never been a "cool kid." Especially in New York City. For those of you who don't know the NYC teenager scene, it's basically a lot of kids with a ton of freedom. New York isn't like any other city. Most of my friends who live in the suburbs couldn't wait to be sixteen to get their license so they could go wherever, whenever. In New York City, kids can basically go anywhere from a really young age because of public transportation and the fact that you can walk pretty much anywhere easily. Because of all of the independence so early on, the teens kind of act like they're in their twenties. Getting into clubs, parties, whatever. It's intense. And I wasn't into that. I was more into staying in my room, writing music and novels. LAWL.

Back then, my best friend was a girl named Katie. At the time, we were inseparable. And we had decided this would be our best Halloween yet. We weren't gonna repeat Halloween 2010, trick-or-treating with her ten-year-old brother and sister. NOPE. WE WERE COOL THIS YEAR.

We spent days figuring out our costumes. She decided to be a cat, and I was a Smurf. The blonde one, DUH.

We had these adorable outfits. BUT . . . living in New York City, the weather is unpredictable. We woke up and heard it was going to be thirty-five degrees. Not exactly a good day for a cute little Halloween outfit.

I had also heard that Dan*, the cute guy I was in love with, was having a party. I just knew we would get invited. My other friend Mandy*—this whole story will become clearer after you read Chapter 15: "Why I Love Unrequited Love"—was going to his party, and she HAD to invite me along . . . right?

Katie and I decided to be nice and take her little brother out trick-or-treating for a few hours before the (inevitable) party. Well, hours passed, her little brother was racking up the candy, and then we both finally got a group text from Mandy.

A SELFIE.

OF HER.

AND DAN.

WHATTTTTT?!!!!

"best night ever <3"

We were shocked. The party was in full swing, Mandy and Dan were hanging out, and Katie and I were now stuck taking her brother house to house to collect Milky Way bars.

Most of the houses started turning off their lights, and the night was growing dim. At 8:30 p.m. we decided to turn in. Katie and I walked sadly into a nearby CVS to get twenty bags of now-discounted Halloween candy. WE ARE ANIMALS. We walked back to her apartment—alone.

We sprawled out in Katie's room, listening to "Skyscraper" by Demi Lovato on repeat, shoveling mini-Crunch bar after mini-Crunch bar into our mouths, while tears of blue mascara (I WAS A SMURF, REMEMBER?) dripped down my face.

THIS WAS TRAGIC.

Katie's mom asked if we wanted anything

because our moms were ordering Chinese food. Sure, we said. Not like we had any cute dresses to fit into for a party or anything.

"I guess we could just write a song?" Katie asked.

"Or have our own party?"

Katie then blasted the ~party anthem~ of the year. LITERALLY. "Party Rock Anthem" by LMFAO.

And then we had a lightbulb idea.

We "accidentally" pocket dialed all of our LAME friends who WERE at that party.

We were screaming and laughing and blasting tons of house music. We were having our own party!

We laughed so hard we cried. We had the best time ever. Then, we tweeted and posted on fb blurry selfies and captioned them "best Halloween after at the craziest exclusive party in Brooklyn <3 #MEMS"

YUP.
WE LIED.
OH WELL.

SUE US

Would you believe it? The next morning all of our "friends" at the party were now inviting US out to hang.

But we remembered, they ONLY invited us out after they thought we were doing something cooler than they were. And that wasn't cool.

So we spent the rest of our nights eating pizza and candy on her floor, writing songs about boys and watching movies.

And if doing that isn't cool, then I don't ever want to be cool.

7

THE TIME RYAN GOSLING GAVE ME A PEP TALK

Let me clarify this by saying I never have met Ryan Gosling. HOWEVER, I frequently watch *Blue Valentine* (which is rated R for a very good reason, so if you aren't seventeen don't watch it because then your parents will hate me for recommending it). It's one of my favorite movies ever, even though it's super depressing because Michelle Williams is life goals (like her clothes, her hair, her acting . . . ugh, just goals). I once watched that film every night for a solid week after a breakup. I figured, I'm already sad, why ruin a good day watching this when I'm happy? I know—weird logic. I watched that movie—and obvi *The Notebook*—over and over again. I love Ryan Gosling so much. So does my mom. She actually thinks she's going to marry him one day. (Sorry, Dad.) We even have matching Ryan Gosling socks. (They are literally socks with a billion pics of Ryan Gosling all over them. Judge me. Don't care.) I even got her a birthday card with a shirtless picture of him on it from that movie *Crazy Stupid Love*. She keeps it on her

nightstand in New Orleans where I'm filming while I'm writing this, so that if people
come over and go into her room she can tell
them that "the photo on the nightstand is a
picture of my husband."

The apple doesn't fall too far from the tree.

(Really so sorry, Dad.)

Also, sorry, Ryan Gosling,
if you ever find out about this.

I'm not a stalker. Really.

Anyway . . . You're probably wondering what
I'm talking about. "You've never met Ryan,
you say, so then how did he give you a pep
talk?"

Let me explain.

You know when you have THOSE days? I'm talking about those days that absolutely suck ass, the days when nothing you put on looks good, when your hair isn't falling the way it's supposed to (no matter how many different tools, curling irons, flat irons, you use), when your eyeliner is just not working out right, when your wings are uneven. Those days when your whole FACE just looks wrong. You're in a bad mood—not sad, not angry, just every little thing is ANNOYING. Maybe the guy you like hasn't texted you back, your salad order came out wrong, there's a HUGE line at Starbucks, your cab driver is rude, you just can't get your FREAKING eyeliner wings to match . . . It's those days when everything just SUCKS.

We all have those days. LORD knows I do. All the time. Some days I sit in my room and sob to Taylor Swift music just to be dramatic and then Snapchat selfies of myself with my mascara running just to be all emo. Other times I go to my friend Jenni's house, and I bake gluten-free pancakes and listen to sad music.

But on my lowest of days, when my friends aren't around to hang out with me, I sink to lower levels . . . What I do had been my little secret until . . .

My friend borrowed my phone and noticed that I had text messages in my recents from

Ryan Gosling, Drake, 💜 Zac Efron, and Joseph Gordon-Levitt. 💚

She immediately said, "OMG, YOU'RE TEXTING RYAN GOSLING?!"

But before I could grab my phone back, she clicked on the chat box and saw it was her messages to me.

That was awkward.

Basically I do this thing sometimes where when I'm really sad I text my friends for advice and when they reply I change their names so it looks like I'm getting messages from hot male celebrities. Then I can read it and think, "Oh my god, Drake is so sweet to send me uplifting quotes." (Usually, this is actually my friend Denise.) Or "OMG, Ryan really doesn't have to send me cute pics of mini-potbellied pigs! That's just too kind." (That's my mom with the pics.) Or "Zac . . . is so clingy sometimes, but so adorbz that he really cares for me." (Summer, of course.)

Yes.
I am insane.

But I'm okay with it.

As far as I'm concerned, anything that helps you get through the day is okay. As long as it's not illegal. (If it's illegal, don't do that. So not worth it.) But THIS ISN'T, damnit. And if I want to have a dream, I damn well WILL.

JUDGE ME. #haterzaremymotivatorz

HOW TO GET OVER A BREAKUP

Whether someone has just broken up with you, or you have broken up with someone, leaving a relationship is never fun. Even the most dysfunctional couples can suffer a sadness that comes with the end of something.

I have been on both ends and neither is easy. I think a lot of the times we think we're supposed to feel better if we're the one who ended things, but what I've learned is that life and love and relationships are way more complicated than that. It's often depicted as the classic "you can't fire me, I quit!" thing but that's not always what it feels like. Sometimes we break up with people because we know that, ultimately, it's the best thing for them or for us, not necessarily because we want to. Doing the right thing is sometimes the hardest thing in the world. No joke.

But this particular chapter is about how to get over someone breaking up with you.

Although, honestly, this advice pretty much applies to everything.

1 It's okay to cry. Like seriously. Crying is really therapeutic. Sometimes I honestly look forward to getting in a nice, good sob. Keeping your emotions bottled up isn't healthy. If you're sad and you wanna cry, do it. Ending a relationship is sucky; waterworks should come. Turn on *The Notebook*, grab a tub of chocolate chip cookie dough ice cream, and go cry your eyes out. It can feel good to be cliché! I guarantee you'll feel better afterward.

2 Write a super-honest letter to your ex, but whatever you do DON'T SEND IT. Write out everything you feel and the reasons why you ended it or why you think they ended it or why you think they're a total a-hole. Unleash all of your feelings, frustrations, and honest sadness. Then burn it or rip it up. Destroy it. (Sometimes the destroying is even more cathartic than the writing.) I know it sounds really cheesy, but I swear it works. Then dance to your favorite breakup song. Right now "Reflections" by MisterWives is the most right.

3 Move on. I know it seems hard and I'm not necessarily a proponent of "the best way to get over someone is to get under someone else" because intimacy breeds feelings and it's a really bad idea to involve someone else in your life if you aren't emotionally ready to let them in. HOWEVER . . . it is healthy to go out and flirt. Go to a party with your friends, and meet guys. Let them buy you dinner or coffee or drinks. This does NOT make you obligated to kiss them or sleep with them or anything with them. Sometimes just knowing that other people are interested in you romantically makes the sting of a breakup a little less painful.

Take time for yourself. This seems like such a duh comment but it's totally true. I hate to sound cheesy, but in order to fall in love with someone or have someone fall in love with you, you have to love yourself first. A lot of times, I have gotten into relationships to feel better about myself. But ultimately that creates so much anxiety and pressure. Before getting involved with someone else again, ask yourself, "Am I doing this because I really like this person, or am I doing this solely because they really like me?" Putting your self-worth in someone else's hands is like putting your life savings into a burglar's pocket. NEVER build your self-esteem on someone else's affirmation of you. Your S.O. should make you a better version of you, not make you who you are.

And at the end of the day, breakups suck. There's no way around it. But the best thing you can do is surround yourself with good music, good food, and good friends, and realize that everything does happen for a reason.

When one door closes . . .

Five other really cute possible suitors walk in?

K, maybe that's wishful thinking. 😬

THE

FRIEND

CODE

Not too long ago I learned about the difference between a big friendship problem and one you should just let slide.

For instance, here's one to let slide:

Your friend "borrows" your hair tie . . . the classic "omg, can I please borrow that? My hair is so freaking long!" Like okay, Noelle, you have nice hair.

Why you gotta make me feel
BAD ABOUT IT?

(I'm not bitter. Love you, Noelle. <3)

But let me tell you right now: YOU ARE NEVER GETTING THAT HAIR TIE BACK. So either invest in a large stock of neutral earth-tone hair ties or don't wear them on your wrist. xo

Yes, there are small friend problems—your friend doesn't answer texts quickly or maybe they're a little needy or maybe they brag a lot. These all fall under the category of "Yeah, they're kind of annoying sometimes."

But then there are big issues—issues that can break even the strongest friendships.

I'm gonna revisit a friend I might have mentioned once or twice before—Summer.

Before London, Summer was my best friend. We told each other literally everything. She was my confidante. I could tell her when I had a massive zit and go into excruciatingly awful detail about how wondrous it was to pop it. I could tell her about that one girl I couldn't stand who passive-aggressively favorited my tweets. I could tell her about the nights when I was really sad and couldn't sleep, and she'd always be there to answer the phone and tell me a joke about the really hot girl who liked my then-crush's Facebook profile picture. I remember the time she told me, "Whoa, are we really stressing about this girl? Like, okay, she's hot, but you're legit ten times hotter. Plus, she looks totally vapid, and you're supersmart and funny and awesome. Relax. He's totally into you."

SIDE NOTE:

I was not hotter than said girl considering she's an ACTUAL model. Like as a profession. So . . . YEAH. But everyone's hot, tbh—just different hot, so go out and be your own form of hot.

SIDE SIDE NOTE:

Said "crush" became my boyfriend, so heyyyyyy, score for ABrez. Holla.

Anyway . . .

Summer could also always talk to me. She'd call me at 2:00 a.m., and we'd sit on Skype for hours, joking and laughing and gossiping and being generally teenager-y and gross.

But I felt our friendship really was the strongest after I went through this one really sad and awful breakup. I mean I was SAD. I wasn't by any means in love with this person, but at the time, that particular relationship meant a lot to me. I was devastated that it wasn't there anymore. Especially since it had ended on such a bad note. VISUALIZE me crying in a cab while listening to Bon Iver and then showing up at my friend Ari's house to vent my sadness into a song. (LOVE YOU, ARI.)

At that time, Summer was totally there for me. She answered my calls at any hour of the night. She talked me through my horror over him finding someone new SO FREAKING

QUICKLY. She recommended chick flicks and sad songs and uplifting songs and told me to work out and drink tea and take care of myself. I mean, she was really THERE when I needed her. And I was always—and to some degree, will always—be grateful to her for that. Cuz at that point in time, what I so desperately needed was someone to tell me,

"You're worth more than what one lame-ass guy thinks of you."

And that's what she told me.

Even then, though, Summer had her quirks.
She was spacey and erratic and slightly flaky.
At the time, I could've called her insane, but
in that insane-but-charming sort of way.

I never saw any of these "quirks" affecting
our friendship negatively.

That was, until she started dating Joel.

Yes, that Joel. The smart, cool British hipster.
The one Summer was so into that she moved
to London just to be with him. She gushed
about how cute he was and all the adorable
texts he'd send her. They were nauseatingly
sweet, especially to a singleton like me.

Once she moved, I messaged Joel to take
care of her, and he promised he would.

I also, in jest, told him to find me a "hot British boyfriend," which he delivered on. (Yeah, Adam!) ;)

But a few weeks after Summer moved, she started acting strange. Sad, I guess. I assumed it was just homesickness. I mean, moving from California to England is a big culture shock. Add in jet lag and not really knowing anyone but one person, it's a lot to absorb. Especially at nineteen.

She swore she was fine and just missed her mom and her dogs and friends back in LA.

Summer seemed to perk up as Adam ("the hot British boyfriend") and I got closer. It was super fun at first. But then I went to visit her in London and after a few days, she started acting sort of shady—canceling plans, being unresponsive and cold. She insisted it wasn't personal; she said she just didn't feel well.

Before I knew it my trip to London was over, and I was heading back to NYC. That day, I found out that Summer was also leaving, three months before she was scheduled to move back to LA. She said she had family things to deal with. This seemed odd to me on many levels.

1. I was her best friend. She told me every-thing. Why wouldn't she have told me this earlier?

2. Why wouldn't she tell her boyfriend? The person she ALSO told everything to.

The whole thing seemed just really strange.

The next few months were a downward spi-ral of her breaking up with Joel, then getting back together, then breaking up again, then making up rumors about me and him and my boyfriend. It was a huge mess. A huge, huge mess I didn't need and one far too com-plicated and tangled to unravel now. That would need a whole separate book in itself.

However, these were all things I thought I could handle. To me all these little dramas fell under the "Well, Summer's just dramatic" category. I let it slide. I wasn't going to just forget that she had been such an amazing friend when I needed one.

But then that changed.

Something happened that really crossed the line. Many lines.

One morning, about four months after we came back from the UK, I found out that Summer had hooked up with my ex—a guy who had ROYALLY screwed me over. I was even willing to let this slide until Summer started trying to explain to me why he wasn't "that bad."

AND IF THAT WASNT THE ULTIMATE

BACKSTAB. Remember that guy she helped me get over?

Well . . .

She became super "close" with him, too.

[
The moral of the story is:
There is a code.
]

And it's different for everyone. There are lines that just cannot be crossed. There are things that are too hard to handle. Things you can't . . . just deal with. And if a friend crosses those boundaries, you have to realize they were never really a friend to begin with.

So look back, enjoy the memories, and just know . . . people cannot be trusted once they have broken the friend code.

Madness
(A She Poem)

"Don't get to know me"
She thought as they kissed
"You'll love me at first but
I'll never be missed
You'll find me intriguing
A prize to be won
But it's always quite certain I'm never the one
The one that will last in your mind as a catch
The one that is easy not stuck in her past
And maybe at first I'll capture your interest
But soon you will see the charm isn't permanent"

"Don't get too close"
She pleaded and begged
He said he would stay
But he'd already left

He took out his anger
In ways and not words
"I thought you would like it"
He said when it hurt

"Manic Pixie Dream Girl"
Clichés were what he resented
As well as where he resided
But I prayed that one day
He'd love who I was
Not just who I'd became
This zombie this model
This, dare I say mannequin
Who nodded, agreed
Only his opinion
This cutout

This magnet
Of things he decided
Of actions and moments
And painful submissions

This guilt and this sadness
That only was fueled by the cruel
twisted madness

"Cuz loves only madness"
She thought as they kissed
That only I'll feel
But he'll never miss

The truth is he loves her

But
She can't quite remember
Cuz the boy she's with now
Wouldn't raise a fist at her
Wouldn't guilt
Wouldn't question
Wouldn't scorn with resentment
Wouldn't make her feel wanted
Then just leave her stranded

Cuz the boy she's with now
Actually loves her
And she's startled
And cautious
But she still loves the difference

10

HOW NOT TO FLIRT: A STEP-BY-STEP GUIDE TO GIVING OFF THE "NAH" VIBE

If you are single, alone, and hoping to find the match of your dreams—a fun, normal, sweet guy with similar interests, hobbies, and sense of humor . . . If you WANT to find an S.O. with potential to be a long-term mate . . .

You are reading the wrong chapter.

In fact, you are probably reading the wrong book and talking to the wrong girl.

In my nineteen years—okay eighteen, but nineteen in like less than a month—of living, I have become an expert, a connoisseur if you will, of how NOT to flirt with people of the opposite gender.

Flirting is a skill, in my opinion. Some people are born naturally seductive and flirtatious.

My mother is mystified by my lack of skills; she swears that at my age she had ALLLLLL the men. LIKE K, MOM, THANKS FOR MAKIN' ME FEEL SINGLE AS A PRINGLE OVER HERE. 😞.

I have friends who can win over guys without doing anything AT ALL. It used to bother me. I'd go out in a group and always be the "little sis" or the "baby" of the group. It's so bad my nickname is actually "baby" (or sometimes "baby spice" when I'm feeling a little 👧).

One evening, I asked my friend Lily to tell me honestly what I was doing wrong. She gave me that sad, sympathetic look that all my friends give me as she told me that I "didn't need to change" myself in order to get guys to like me. Before I tell you what I think about that statement, let's first go through some of the things I have done (and admittedly still do from time to time) that have led me to want to share my hard-won wisdom about how NOT to flirt.

1. Here's how NOT to start a conversation:

"Hey, there. I just stepped in my cat's hair ball. How are you 😊?"

Yes. That is a direct quote from me. And yes. I am ashamed.

While some folks might find my cat's bodily functions and my lack of attention to the carpet charming, others might find it, idk, DISGUSTING. I told my friend Noelle about this, and she immediately told me to punch myself in the face for my severe stupidity. I didn't and you shouldn't either, but she had a point. Noelle is one of my best and oldest friends. Not like, she's old, she's only a year older than me, but I've known her forever. She's brutally honest, loud, and aggressive in the best way. If I ever went to jail, I'd call Noelle to bail me out. She'd probably walk in and say, "Let's go, you dumb whore," and scream at me, but never tell another soul. That's why I love her.

Here's perhaps a better conversation starter:

"Hey, did you hear Mumford & Sons is releasing a new album? Mentally preparing myself for all the feels."

Band is interchangeable, but at least it's something he can react to. At least it's something you'd both want to talk about—unlike stepping in cat hair balls, which, let's face it, less said about cat hair balls in general, the better. Anyway, the conversation will go even better if you make sure it's a band or movie or book or whatever that you BOTH like. If you just look through his likes on fb and choose something randomly, chances are you're gonna look really dumb when he starts asking you questions and you have NOTHING. I have done this many a time, most notably when I was fifteen and a guy I liked (who my friends and I refer to as "Voldemort" but "Voldi" for short) told me he was really into dubstep.

At the time, I thought he was the sun, the stars, and the moon and all that was holy in the world, so naturally when he talked about deadmau5 and Modestep, I pretended to know exactly what he was talking about. I thought I'd be cool and prove that I knew my stuff (which I didn't), and proceeded to spend the rest of the night researching different dubstep artists. I really liked "Promises" by Skrillex when I listened to it on YouTube, probably cuz it was the most pop one I could find. (I was fifteen—DON'T HATE.) I posted the link to the lyric video on Facebook that night so that he would see it and realize I had been a dub fan way before I knew he was into it, too. Then he'd know that I definitely wasn't pretending to like it just to impress him (which I totally was, but yeah). I wasn't surprised when I woke up in the morning to see he had commented on the link. *Nailed it,* I thought.

That was until I noticed that his comment linked to a meme that said, "If the only dubstep artist she knows is Skrillex, she's too young for you, bro."

WHICH WAS RICH CUZ HE WAS YOUNGER THAN ME—BUT OK, SASS.

Sorry for that long tangent. I APOLOGIZE, but I'm still not over it. ¯_(ツ)_/¯

---

2. When getting ready for a date, look at yourself in the mirror. Pay close attention to your outfit.

Are you wearing black jeans with a long sweater and boots? CUTE. YOU'RE KILLIN' IT, BABE. WORK IT.

Now are you pairing it with a gigantic cat bag? And by cat bag I mean, a bag with a cat's face on it? Does your wallet have a smiling pug on it? Is your phone case a kitten in an ice cream cone that says "'Sup?'"? Yes?

K.

Probably not a great way to accessorize for a first date, right?

HOW DO I KNOW? THESE ARE THINGS I HAVE WORN OUT ON DATES. I admit to using said cat bag, but that was because I was going to the gym before the date, and I'm allowed to do whatever I want if I am going to work out. I deserve it.

Here's the thing: Individually, quirky accessories can seem cute, endearing, even hilarious. There is a time and a place for the cat bag, pug wallet, and kitten phone case . . . But paired together on a date, especially a FIRST date, it screams ISSUES. I'm all for freedom of expression through clothes, and think it's rad to own it totally—cuz confidence IS sexy!—HOWEVER, unless you met him at the local animal shelter, you probably don't want to lead with "I'm obsessed with baby animals and like to wear photos of them on my body at all times."

Let him get to know how cool you are first and THEN let him see how your adorable wallet companion is just ~killing~ the game.

---

3. Talking about pregnancy with a guy you like but haven't even been on a date with yet is something I am very PRO at.

Okay. Let me explain.

Sometimes, I think I am the most hilarious person I know. Sometimes, I KNOW I am.

What can I say? I crack myself up. ¯_(ツ)_/¯

But sometimes over text my hilariousness doesn't come across quite the way I want it to. Example:

I'm at work. It's late. I'm tired and have had way too many espressos because it was 2:00 a.m. and I was working and ALSO cuz I'd just learned how to use the espresso machine on set and liked doing it in front of people to prove how skilled I was. And let me tell you: There really is a difference between being ALERT and being AWAKE. I was so jacked-up on caffeine that I was not thinking rationally.

So, I'm talking to this guy. Let's just call him Jake. He's being really sweet and funny, and I feel like I'm doing a GREAT job at being flirtatious. Until . . . he told me his crush on me was "unwavering" and I decided a good reply would be:

> "OMG, you're making me nauseous.
> But, like, in a good way.
> Like when you're pregnant and you
> have morning sickness, but it's okay
> cuz you know you'll have a baby,
> eventually."

Why, Abbie? Why?!?

He didn't talk to me the rest of the night.

But the next day, he did so it's all good—dwai dwai.

Also another thing not to joke about over text—herpes. Don't ever mention herpes in writing. That's a bad call. Example taken from MY LIFE YET AGAIN! smh.

Cute normal nice boy: "I'm just hanging out. Drinking a dope milk shake. Too bad you're not here; we could share it. 😔 "

Me being an absolute menace to society: "Ya, except too bad I have herpes sorry :/"

No reply.

Me: "Hahaha. I'm totally kidding. I swear I don't really have herpes."

Me three hours later: "Okay, so I can see how that whole thing earlier wasn't funny and was kinda terrifying, but yeah I def don't have herpes."

Me two days later: "Hey, just making sure U don't hate me. LOL. I swear I don't have herpes."

Me nine thousand years later alone with 876 cats: "I still don't have herpes. Just a lot of cats. Does the milk shake offer still stand or nah?"

Don't ever joke about pregnancy or herpes over text. Ever. Just. Just don't. TRUST ME.

And finally:

---

4. Telling guys why they SHOULDN'T date me is possibly my best skill.

Maybe it's a self-preservation thing. That's probably what a therapist would say, and maybe that's right. I've definitely had my fair share of guys who have been less than Noah from *The Notebook* status. And that's being HIIIIIIGHLY generous. My approach in the past has been, "Okay, I am annoying and awful and I spend all of my time on Tumblr and watching sad movies. I'm obsessed with Christmas, and I love my cat more than any other human. I am really not the romantic type, and I am probably not that hot to you or not your type and definitely not worthy of hanging out with all the time, so you should probably just leave right now." And I use that, I guess, as a way to say, "HEY, I really like you, and I really want you to like me, too, and I need you to reassure me that you like me right now so I'm gonna tear myself apart and tell you everything I don't like about myself so you know it and don't get freaked out by it when eventually it comes out."

But I have come to realize that if a guy asks you out, if he wants to spend a lot of time with you, talking to you, initiating conversation, if you have good talks and times and you feel good around him, he likes you. And he's probably seen A LOT of the things you're insecure about and not even noticed them (or maybe he even—gasp!—likes them).

One time, after being with a guy for a really long time, I told him I was really insecure about my laugh because it's kinda loud and not very cute—like, idk, how so many girls look gorgeous when they laugh but I look like I'm having a stroke. And you know what he said? He said that was one of his favorite things about me. And yeah, okay, whatever, right? Like, of COURSE he's saying that. But then he showed me a text he had sent his friend the night we had met saying how "cute" my laugh was. CUTE? MY LAUGH?? I promise you it is the furthest thing from cute. But if someone really likes you, REALLY genuinely likes you, the things you dislike about you can be lovable to them. And no one likes someone who is constantly hating on the things they love.

So . . . What is my opinion on what Lily had said about me not having to change myself to get guys to like me?

SHE'S RIGHT. I don't. And I won't ever again.

Well. Maybe I will. Who knows? I'm still young, and I could do something stupid like I did with Voldi again if, say, Zac Efron called up, like, "Hey, girl, wanna go see this cool new reggae band tonight?" And I'd be like, "Oh my God, Zac, I don't know how you got my number considering we met once and I sobbed. I thought you'd be creeped out, but okay, yeah, I love reggae. Let's do it."

But. The chances of that happening are like . . . . IT'S NOT GONNA HAPPEN, ABS. IT'S JUST NOT.

The point is: You shouldn't ever change yourself to fit someone else's ideal perfect girl. The older I get the more I realize there isn't a perfect girl and there isn't a perfect boy. You can meet someone and think everything they say and do has been sent down by angels and unicorns. You can think you'll never get sick of them ever and you'll have a beautiful life together filled with morning cups of coffee and nights of eating pizza on fire escapes and making out and being perfectly perfect together, and I HATE bursting that bubble for you but you do get sick of them. After a while the little things you found cute can become weirdly obnoxious. Like why the F do you need to YAWN SO LOUDLY? But whatever. Maybe he'll stop doing that or try to. And you'll try to change things that annoy him, like hogging the blanket while you're Netflixing on the couch. These are small changes you make when you are ALREADY in a relationship. But you should never fundamentally change things about yourself that are inherently YOU. Ever. ESPECIALLY to impress a guy enough to ask you on a date. That's CRAZY talk. But . . . that also doesn't mean you have to be a full-blown psychopath as I may have been in the past. There's a time and a place to carry the cat bags, kids.

And there ya have it, folks. Feel free to refer to this anytime you want to know what NOT to say to your crush. Or what to say if a guy you DON'T like is hitting on you. Then you can hit him with the whole cat hair ball thing. And if it doesn't bother him . . .

Well . . .

He might be a keeper

11

BASICS

Whether you have been dumped, or you have been the dumper, it's safe to say that breakups are never fun. And if you are the one person in the entire universe that got through a breakup completely and 100 percent unscathed then . . .

1. CONGRATS!

2. You're lying.

Ending a relationship is awful and horrible and heartbreaking and gut-wrenching, and there's no way of getting around that. I mean, you're basically telling someone you've potentially loved, or at least cared a great deal about, that you don't want him in your life anymore. And we can all use that "we can stay friends" line until we are blue in the face, but NOBODY likes hearing that almost as much as no one likes saying it. You can almost never go backward happily. There really is no GOOD breakup.

Now if you have just broken up with someone and you are currently sobbing onto this page and/or considering chucking this book across your room and curling into a ball of sadness for eternity, FEAR NOT! I am not just here to be a total downer. I have tips! I'm here to guide you through it! I have NUGGETS OF BREAKUP WISDOM. That's right. It's going to be okay. ABrez is here to help.

Let's start at the top. Let's start with the scenario that you are the one being broken up with.

The most common thing I hear from my friends is, "I never saw it coming." And that can be true. Sometimes you don't even notice when someone is pulling away, but there are ALWAYS signs.

1 He starts acting distant. Sometimes it's not even as obvious as ignoring texts or canceling plans. Sometimes, you just can feel him starting to pull away. It's the less eye contact, more time on his phone, not paying as much attention to what you're saying. It may seem insignificant—and maybe it is—but sometimes it's not.

2 He invites friends to all of your hangouts. Or, as I like to call it—"buffers." Maybe you've been arguing a little bit, and he feels awkward hanging out completely alone. BUT that's not a way to solve the problem. Having a bunch of people around when things already aren't ideal is just a way for him to avoid his issues. DON'T let him get away with this. Maybe try saying, "Hey, I know things haven't been as great as usual lately, maybe we should just have a one-on-one night so we can really talk everything through so we're both happy. I get uncomfortable talking about these kinds of things in front of other people." That way, you're getting your point across while also not putting the blame on him.

3 You just get that VIBE. Sometimes, nothing is really different. He's calling, texting, telling you he loves you. He keeps his word with plans. But you still feel like something is "off." It can make you feel crazy sometimes, because you don't have any concrete issues. Things just feel weird. Trust your gut. Your gut is usually right. If you feel like something's wrong, if you're anxious and unhappy, it's worth bringing up. Try saying, "I don't wanna be 'that girl' but, is it me or are things kind of off between us lately? Maybe we can grab coffee and talk about it? I know I always think more clearly after a good pumpkin spice latte." Best case, it's nothing and you laugh about it later. Worst case, there is something going on, but at least then it's out in the open. Better to be sad than to think you're crazy.

Talking in person about issues is ALWAYS ideal. Second best is over the phone. Texting really isn't an option when it comes to stuff like this. Too much room for misinterpretation. He may say things like, "I get awkward over the phone" or "I can really pay more attention over text" but that is, tbh, bull. If he won't meet up with you in person or at the very least call you to make things right, turn his notifications to "DO NOT DISTURB" on your phone until he calls you. Best to keep a friend around during this so he or she can make sure you don't sneak a peek at his messages.

And finally, here are some things that you SHOULDN'T worry about:

1 He texts less. This is something every girl freaks out about sometimes, but, tbh, once you've been in a relationship for a little bit, neither of you NEEDS constant communication to know that you're still really into one another. Try to relax. Talk to your friends before you confront him, cuz it really sucks when things are going good and your paranoia causes you to do that whole, "Why aren't u texting me as much? Don't U like me anymore? lol?"

NOT THAT I'VE DONE THAT OR ANYTHING.

2 He's not super lovey-dovey anymore. Idk, maybe he uses your pet name less frequently or maybe he isn't constantly stroking your hand across the table. As long as he isn't acting super cold and shady, don't freak. This is normal. It's called moving out of the Honeymoon Phase. The Honeymoon Phase is where everything is ideal and perfect and you're super obsessed with the other person. This usually lasts about a month or two. It's actually a good thing when it ends cuz it means you're just entering a new, even closer part of your relationship. RELAX.

3 He forgets your, I DUNNO, four-month anniversary or something. Guys RARELY pay close attention to the details. I once asked my ex if he remembered when we started dating (in March) and he said "like end of April or something." I remember getting pissed off, but honestly, he knew it was in the spring so I let it slide. Forgetting a few details doesn't necessarily mean that he's not into you anymore.

Now, let's say you are the one ENDING the relationship. THIS SUCKS, TOO. You cared about this person at one point. There's probably things about your S.O. you still care about. There's nothing fun about breaking someone's heart.

1 Really think about why you're ending it before you end it. Rash decisions aren't a good idea. Maybe try taking a break. Start with something like, "We've been arguing a lot lately. Why don't we spend a week or two by ourselves to cool off and think, and then we can get back together to discuss things when we're both a little less heated?"

He may get pissed off, but taking a break is a really great way to spend time alone and see if you really are happier without that person in your life. Especially if you've been fighting a lot. A little time and distance will help you see if what you've been arguing about is temporary or something that's really wrong with your relationship.

If you decide the break you're on should be permanent, expect him to be angry. Try to be as gentle as possible when ending it. Take responsibility. Focus on the positives. You're not trying to destroy him, right? It's not an argument to be won, just a thing that needs to be said. I can't tell you exactly what to tell him, because I don't know your relationship. Only you know what that person would benefit most from hearing. Also, realize there is no way for you to be totally comforting without giving the other person false hope, which is really not nice, even if you only have good intentions. Expect them to yell and curse and maybe say things that are hurtful. Try not to take it personally, but also don't be a doormat. You don't have to sit there and let them tear into you. Find a way to say something like, "I get that you're hurt and upset, and I'm sorry. But I think a lot of what you're saying is fueled by anger, and for my own sanity, I need to go now." Also, try to avoid as best you can dumping someone in public or by text. In public, they don't have the license to really feel their emotions, and it's just a way for you to feel less awkward cuz you know they can't be as upset in front of total strangers. Over text is just . . . No.

3 Realize you don't need a definitive reason to get out of a situation. If you're with someone and unhappy, that's good enough. You don't have to wait for him to cheat on you or be a jerk. You don't need

documentable cause. I've ended things with people where they've been great, but I'm just personally not happy. There is no reason to stay with someone if you aren't happy—and don't EVER let someone manipulate you into staying for THEIR happiness. There's a great quote from a book, I forget which one, but it says, "You are not required to set yourself on fire in order to keep other people warm." REMEMBER THAT.

ALSO. AFTERWARD, don't move on till you're ready. Sometimes, you want to find someone new right away, but that's usually a bad idea. If you're still hung up on your ex (and there's a good chance you are), then it's unfair to you AND the new person to involve them in your life if you're not ready to be emotionally available for them.

At the end of the day, breakups are iehgvud-fgid (that's the sound of my head pounding on the keyboard) awful. But in either scenario, you will survive—and so will the other person, which may be an even tougher pill to swallow. Right? Just cuz you've moved on and found someone else, doesn't mean you want him to move on, too. Sad truth: We all want to be the best thing you ever had. So, when you're feeling a bit jealous, like it was a bit too easy for him, refer back to Chapter 1: Reasons to Not Stalk Your Ex. UNFRIEND THEM. IGNORE THEM. Why put yourself through the agony of seeing them with someone else—even if you know it shouldn't be agony at all?

And when all else fails, and you start to backslide and doubt your decision or you start to think that one sad text or funny fb post will win him back, put on your favorite movie, call your friends over, have a dance party, cry as much as you want to sad music, and eat tons and tons of chocolate.

And KNOW you will survive and that eventually you will really be ready to move on.

WHY NOT TO BELIEVE EVERYTHING YOU READ ON SOCIAL MEDIA

12

I am a product of the internet era. I have grown up with cell phones, Wi-Fi, and social media. I got my first phone when I was ten, a Virgin Mobile phone. My parents set it up so I could only make emergency calls—to 911 and to them. But I still found a way to text my cousin about *The O.C.* Yes, I have grown up in the time when everything I could possibly need was a click away. I'm so thankful for that. It makes life easy.

However, sometimes I wish I was born in, like, 1889. Technology, although brilliant, is terrifying. And daunting. And nerve-racking.

Social media has become a beast. Everyone has a voice. There're no filters. No editors. No adult in the room. It can be a horrifying outlet for angry people to vent their frustration on the world—anonymously.

Except, NO ONE is really anonymous.

strange concept, no?

In a world where your name can be anything you choose, you are still not an unknown entity.

Everyone is a celebrity, and anyone you know could be the paparazzi.

I know friends who have not gotten accepted to colleges because a photo of them ~schwasted~ at a bar was posted on Facebook. THIS IS REAL.

How does this happen, though? How does Surfcutie90's post get seen by a dean at Harvard? It's simple as this:

Type in ANY name you can think of. You are bound to see something you DON'T want to. It's bad for anyone. Whether you are

Angelina Jolie, or a middle school student in Iowa, you may be subject to unknown photos and misplaced quotes.

I have known this my whole life. But it only came to a head recently.

I woke up one morning while I was in London, and did what most people do when they first wake up. I reached over to my nightstand and picked up my phone. I scrolled through Facebook posts with blurry eyes, semiconsciously liking some cousin of mine's best friend's wife who got engaged to some guy who works at Bank of America! MAZEL TOV!

Then I switched to Twitter, scrolled through, favorited some relatable tweets about what it feels like to see your crush flirting with another girl, and also saw that my friend Timothy had retweeted my pic of an otter playing with a Frisbee. #TOOREAL

THENNNN I switched to Instagram, liked a bunch of my friends' pictures, mostly selfies toasting with chai lattes or the occasional OOTD post. CUTE.

Then I checked my texts—nothing. Okay. MOVING ON.

This was all standard routine for me. And the final part of the routine: The Underground.

The Underground is a place some of my friends and I have created as a sort of "safe social media space." A lot of my friends are known to some degree whether they are actors/singers/YouTubers. And sometimes we can't say everything we want to say on our public Twitters because our publicists would murder us. We create dumb names for our usernames and post about everything openly. When I first got on the Underground, I thought it was so fun but after a while I realized how toxic it was. Instead of being a place where we could, idk, say the F-word (gasp) and feel cool and edgy, it became a place where we could gossip about one another in a way we couldn't publicly. It became less and less fun and more and more cliquey and catty.

Anyway . . . I went onto the Underground and was immediately bombarded by a plethora of tweets. Before being able to read them coherently, all I could make out was "DID ABBIE KNOW?"

Joel started calling my phone. I answered and he said, voice shaky, "Have you been on the Underground yet?"

To silence, he added,

"Don't do it."

I hung up and scrolled through as many tweets as I could possibly find. All I could figure out was that Summer had hung out with someone, and I would be mad about it.

Who on earth could she have hung out with,
I thought. I'm pretty chill about most things.
And I definitely wouldn't tell someone they
aren't allowed to hang out with someone.

THAT IS . . .

until I came across THE PHOTO.

The pic was of Summer with my ex. YEAH. It
was weird. They had their arms around each
other; it was really strange. I didn't understand why this was happening. And because
I was in London again, I couldn't even reach
her for a comment on it. All I knew then was
everyone was talking about it.

"I heard they hooked up in the bathroom."

"I HEARD he proposed to her, and she said
hell nah."

"I SAW THEM TALKING IN THE COR-
RIDOR REALLLLLLY CLOSE TO EACH

OTHER."

"I heard he was gonna take her to Vegas!!!!!!"

My stomach was turning. How could Summer do this to me? HOW? She's supposed to be my friend!

I was confused and angry and ultimately told Summer, "We are done. You have broken The Friend Code."

You know the friend code. Things friends just don't do to friends. BIG things. Fundamental things. Things that once broken cannot be fixed.

These are not the she's ALWAYS ten minutes late, or she flaked out on plans last minute, or that she's overdramatic, or she forgets to bring back that T-shirt she borrowed after she accidentally spilled green boba tea all over her own shirt . . . Those are little things that, for a real friend, you let slide. But then there are bigger issues. Issues that are inherently wrong. And for me, one of those was . . . Look. You're a pretty girl, you can make out with any guy you want. Why do you have to choose the ONE person that you knew would hurt me the most? Obviously, I'm all about "you can't fight how you feel," but this was deeper. Can't you fight liking the ONE person in the whole world I would beg you NOT to like?

{ BUT PLOT TWIST: }

They didn't hook up. Okay, yes, I wasn't there. I cannot say for 100 percent certain what exactly happened. BUT . . . I choose to believe in the good in people. Call me crazy.

After seeing Summer again for the first time since that whole fiasco, I remembered that I know as well as anyone how words and pictures can be taken out of context. Turns out, Summer was at a party and he was there. He was actually asking her about me. They took a group selfie with each other and posted it on Twitter. The lovely kids on the Underground decided to crop it to make it look very "cuddly."

She assured me she would never ever do that—and neither would he.

I've always said to people, "You can't believe everything you read," and I've always meant that about the gossip pages and professional media. But, after this happened, I realized you can't even believe everything that's said—even when you know the people saying it. A picture on Facebook doesn't PROVE anything. Things can be misunderstood or manipulated. People make assumptions. And the story winds up SOOOOO far away from what actually happened. And the best thing to do if something like this happens, if you hear about something that feels absolutely

UNBELIEVABLE, is go to the source RIGHT AWAY. Tell your friend what you've heard, show her the evidence, and let her explain herself. Then take some time and really carefully think about what you read and what she said—and make up your own mind.

Summer and I ended up talking everything through and now are back to being twin flames again.

In short, kids, decide what you can and can't handle in a friendship, don't believe everything you read on Twitter, and eat your vegetables.

13

WHY BEING HONEST SUCKS A LOT OF THE TIME

Have you ever lied?

> I HAVE TO TELL THE
> TRUTH CUZ THIS IS A
> BOOK AND BOOKS ARE
> SUPER SERIOUS AND
> HONEST.

And the truth is: We've all lied. All of us. Sometimes it's just a little white lie, like when your friend tries on a really awful pair of shoes that don't necessarily make HER look bad but it's just . . . personally . . . nah.

If you don't like them you are allowed to say, "Yeah, they're great!" And it's not necessarily a lie. HOWEVER. If they make HER look bad, it is your friend duty to tell her, "Wellllll, I think you can find something more flattering."

But sometimes, that's hard. You don't want to hurt her feelings. And sometimes your good intentions end up making things worse.

But if telling a friend her boots aren't cute is hard, imagine what it's like when something serious comes up.

I consider myself an honest person. Given the choice, I'll tell the truth. But I've had serious instances when telling the truth felt like the worst thing ever. Once, I was told by a good friend of mine, someone I really trusted, let's call her Charlotte, that my friend Mandy's boyfriend was cheating on her.

My head was spinning, my stomach turning. It brought up bad memories. I've been cheated on in the past—and it sucked. I hated thinking that Mandy would suffer the same agony. It didn't seem right or fair—and I didn't want it to be true.

But after hearing from a bunch of people different tales of his "indiscretions," I went with Charlotte and met Mandy at Starbucks. Charlotte and I were totally over-caffeinated and immediately began rambling on, maybe not as gently as we should have, about what we had heard. Mandy took it all in; her face was stoic and still. When our hyper-ness wore off and we had told her all there was to tell, Mandy burst into tears. Not sobs, just tears. Which was almost worse than her screaming at us and cursing us out.

To be fair, I get it. I honestly was so freaked out by the whole situation that I didn't take the time I should have to break it to her slowly. It's like when you get home late from a party and your parents start yelling at you, "DO YOU GET HOW WORRIED I WAS? DO YOU UNDERSTAND? YOU'RE GROUNDED." But they aren't really mad; they're just worried. Worry can come off as really aggressive even when you don't mean it to be. Not saying this is exactly the same, but I was really worried and I didn't handle it as well as I could have.

She stood up and stared at us both. She said it simply wasn't true and then just left. I felt SO bad. Was I too honest or was it just the way I'd delivered the news? All I'd wanted to do was protect Mandy from the hurt I had felt when I found out I was cheated on and now it seemed like I had hurt her even worse.

I tried all day to call her but she wasn't answering. Finally, we met up again a couple days later, and she explained to me there was a part of the story that I had swept under the rug. For her, that secret had been most hurtful.

Ya see, what I didn't tell you (or her, at first) was that once Charlotte and I heard that Mandy's bae may have been fooling around, we went on a mission.

WE BECAME SPIES.

Okay. So not literally, obvs, cuz that'd take like a ton of training and work, BUT we did go to his favorite hangout spot and wore all black and watched from another table and . . . yeah. Nothing happened. No secret rendezvous with a raven-haired vixen. Just him. With his bros. Drinkin' lattes.

But still, we had heard SO many stories. I guess Mandy just felt betrayed that we'd sink to that level of stalkerness without even telling her first. But honestly, I was just trying to figure these things out on my own. I didn't want to just take someone else's word for it if I could find out for myself. I don't know. I guess I can be a tad controlling at times, but I honestly was trying to do the right thing. She told me that a lot of the things we heard were just rumors. Nothing more.

I remember when I first heard my ex had cheated.

It happened about two years ago. I was sort of seeing this guy. It wasn't a super-intense relationship, but it felt meaningful to me.

He was living in LA, and I live in NYC, so it was kind of hard but not the worst long-distance thing considering how often I'm in LA for work. I had point-blank asked him if we were boyfriend and girlfriend, and he said, "I don't want to put labels on it, but I promise you I'm not seeing anyone else." Yet another case of a Non-relationship Relationship. I was younger then so I didn't know this wasn't really an acceptable arrangement for me. A lot of people are fine with just casually dating, and that's cool, but for me at that time, it wasn't. And I should've told him that. But I liked him SO much and didn't want to seem clingy.

That relationship came to a head when my friend Mara called me and asked me to meet her for lunch in NYC. I did, and as soon as I sat down, she told me that my non-boyfriend boyfriend was hooking up with one of her friends. At first I didn't believe it, even though Mara is a trustworthy friend. I guess it was denial. But then a ton of other people confirmed it, including the girl Mara had told me about. It sucked, and it made me feel really bad about myself for a long time. To be honest, I still have trust issues from time to time as a result. It's one of those things you never want to have to live through.

SO KIDS . . . HERE'S THE LESSON: There are always rumors. I mean, sometimes mine are in magazines and I need to call my grandma and tell her to NOT read *Us Weekly* this week. (TRUE STORY.) But at the end of the day, rumors are rumors. If you hear something from enough people that you feel you need to tell your friend, you should do it. But maybe don't treat it like it's actual evidence unless you have evidence. And maybe you should really think first about how you should tell your friend this news. Probably rambling on over coffee as if it's juicy gossip is not the best way. I learned that lesson the hard way for sure. Maybe starting out with something like, "Hey, I've been hearing things from a bunch of our friends about your boyfriend maybe not being totally faithful to you. I don't know for sure if it's true, but the sources are legit. Again, I don't wanna spread rumors if they aren't true, but I had to tell you because you're my friend and I want to make sure you're being treated the way you should be. Wanna meet for coffee and talk about it?"

That way you aren't bombarding your friend with this intense news in an alarmed manner. They'll be more willing to accept the conversation and listen and think it through clearly if they don't feel they're being attacked.

As an actor I can confidently say, it's all in the delivery!

Okay. Well. Maybe not everything. But. Yeah. **You get the point.**

#actorjokefail?

UNBE-
WEAVE-
ABLE

Never
—and I mean NEVER—
trust a forty-dollar weave.

Let's start by saying I used to have perfect hair. Like Tumblr-worthy hair. Hair that would get PROB eight thousand reblogs— and that's me being HUMBLE.

But because of my job, a lot of times I'm required to dye it. And, as it turns out, bleaching your hair from auburn to white-blonde five times a year doesn't really help the whole mermaid look.

So, about a year ago, I was stuck wearing clip-in extensions to make my hair look longer than its shoulder-length status. They were nice clip-ins, but I always felt awkward wearing them, like someone could see the actually clips poking through. 'TWAS especially embarrassing when I started dating

Adam. He was always having to fix my hair to cover the clips.

But the bonded-on ones (which I use now) are really expensive so you need to realllllllly invest in them. They do look the realest, tho.

Anyway. The Point: When I saw Summer in London, her hair looked FLAWLESS—LIKE FLAWWWWWLESSSS. It was long and luscious and just . . . yeah . . . PERF.

So I asked her what extensions she was using, and she told me it was a WEAVE. A sewn-in weave. I was skeptical at first—like does that mean it sews into my SCALP?!?

THE HORROR.

It doesn't—jsyk.

She told me her friend did it for her, and it only cost like forty bucks. So I said if she could hook me up with this person, I would love it.

Summer took me to her "salon," which was actually this person's apartment. She was really cool actually and did a great job on it.

At first.

Problem was I was so busy admiring my new gorg locks that I completely didn't listen to any of the maintenance rules she told me.

I JUST WANTED TO TAKE
SELFIES.

After a few weeks, the tracks started to become SUPER noticeable, and my hair became super lifeless. It started looking like random strands of long hair in a gigantic nest (if that makes any sense). I tried every-thing to fix it. Different products, different tools—nothing worked. So finally I called Summer. She said I had to go back every three weeks to get it tightened. See, had I not been so focused on all the Instagram opportunities my new hair would grant me, I would have HEARD the girl tell me this.

Well . . . problem was that now I was back in NYC and couldn't get to London to get the girl to tighten my weave.

So I had to deal with this nest-head of hair for another month.

This is a life lesson, people. Listen up. Moral of the story: IF YOU GET SOMETHING SEWN INTO YOUR HEAD, PUT DOWN YOUR PHONE FOR THREE MINUTES TO MAKE SURE YOU UNDERSTAND WHAT YOU HAVE TO DO TO MAKE SURE IT STAYS ON YOUR HEAD.

(But hey,
at least it inspired me
to check out many cute
hat prospects?)

15

WHY I LOVE UNREQUITED LOVE

Let's flash back to Abba Brez at age four-teen. Lonely. Bored. Not a huge social life. Newly blonde hair that still has streaks of red velvet cupcake–colored strands. Listens to Regina Spektor alone in her room while painting her nails dark blue.

WHAT.

A.

CATCH.

When I was fourteen, I believed there was no such thing as love. I thought, *Guys say they love girls because they want sex* and *Girls say they love guys because they're insecure.*

I was a very opinionated fourteen-year-old.

I was also quite wrong.

I didn't believe I would ever find anyone who could capture my interest enough to make me feel this so-called "magical" feeling. What even was love? Was it even a real emotion?

I had just booked this cool movie and decided to go to dinner with the cast. It was uptown: Sixty-Third and Columbus to be exact. (Yes, I still remember. . . .)

I remember spending a lot of time on my eye makeup because I wanted to seem mature. I showered and used a really expensive body wash from Lush and then put on a Dior eye shadow that I'd gotten for Christmas. It was dark brown and made me feel sophisticated. I wore my favorite jeans, a Free People tank top, and a long cardigan. (It's weird how well I remember this.) Anyway, I told my mom and she told me that my friend and I (let's call her Gwen) couldn't go alone. So my mom and her mom sat at another table. (I KNOW, I WAS MORTIFIED.) Gwen and I got there and met the guys. Let's call them Oliver and Dan. Oliver was muscular and beachy with long blond hair and model-esque features. Dan was tall, lanky, and awkward. And as soon as Dan shook my hand . . .

I fell in love.
HARD.

I had never felt that type of feeling before. This all-consuming, all-encompassing warmth all over my body. Everything he said was hysterical to me. Every time he looked at me, my heart rate would LITERALLY speed up. Every single time I thought about him, I'd smile. What was this? How was this real?

As the night came to a close, Dan gave me

his number and told me how excited he was to start filming. I'd never felt like this. I'd never been this anxious to be on any set.

The next morning when he texted me, I thought I could be happy just staring at his name on my phone forever. I didn't even need to read the text. I had turned into one of THOSE girls that has 😍😍😍😍 that look on her face all the time.

But, even tho I felt so strongly for him, I never wanted to let on. Anytime anyone asked me I'd say, "No way! We are just friends." Which was true. We were. TO MY INFINITE SADNESS.

I didn't want to risk anyone telling him and making things awkward, because I liked him so much. I didn't want anything to jeopardize us talking.

As we worked together, I really felt like he liked me. He always said how great my hair was. Which was weird, but also nice, I guess? Idk? And he always said I looked beautiful. It was more attention than any other guy had ever given me.

Let's be real. I was an awkward, pale, alarmingly small girl (as I still am). Not many guys are lined up around the block for that. But he made me feel like, they SHOULD BE. He made me proud of my awkwardness.

One night, me, Gwen, Oliver, and Dan all went to Gwen's house. We ordered pizza and sat on her bedroom floor talking about life and exes. I had no experience in relationships so I just made shit up. DUH. He, on the other hand, talked about his ex like she was the sun and the stars. It made me melt for him even more. The way he said he'd do anything for her made me feel like he was a genuine catch.

I never felt more obsessed with a human's

soul before. I really liked HIM. And not for his looks or his career but just because he was so fun to be around. He was funny and witty as hell. And sweet and caring and adorable.

Then.

The nightmare began.

I came to work the next day, completely high off of his compliments and the texts he would send me. Even if all he said was hi, the fact that his name showed up on my phone threw me into euphoria.

I walked on set, saw him, and said hi.

He gave me a huge hug and told me I looked beautiful. After I said thank you, he moved aside to reveal this gorgeous, brunette, Brazilian model. Let's call her Amber. I said hi and Dan said, "This is my girlfriend, Amber."

GIRL-FRIEND?! WHAT

My heart fell all the way past my feet and to the underground where Satan himself stabbed it over and over.

With a knot in my throat I just couldn't swallow, I tried to smile.

"Nice to meet you!" I exclaimed.

"I've heard so much about you!" I said, although I'd heard nothing of her.

Was this how Dan was to everyone? Did we ever have a special connection? Or was he just that intensely interested in every girl?

And AMBER?! How did he just not mention he had a gorgeous Brazilian model for a girl-friend?!?

As soon as the polite introductions were through, I headed back to my dressing room. Gwen followed me there, but I locked myself in the bathroom to sob. I didn't want her to know how sad I was.

Eventually stopped crying. I understood why he wanted Amber. She was flawless. I just thought I meant something to him, for some reason.

I spent the next year pining after him.

Praying he would realize what he was missing and would fall in love with me. When he broke up with Amber, I even fought over him with another friend. Until I realized . . .

He didn't want either of us.

That was the hardest pill to swallow.

Sometimes, you think you have this great connection with someone. And sometimes (maybe even most of the time) you're right.

But sometimes that connection is one-sided.

That's what we call unrequited love.

And it sucks. It's agony.

Unrequited love makes you feel like your heart has been ripped out, chopped up, and fed to a dog.

But here's the weird thing: It's also worth-while.

When you're in the throes of unrequited love, it seems impossible to EVER move on. How could you want someone else the way you want them?

But in some ways these are the kindest loves. You have nothing to lose. The relation-ship can be anything you can imagine. No one's heart will really be broken because it's not really real. Well, okay, that's not entirely true. If you really liked someone, that's a feel-ing. You felt that. And no one can take it away from you. Whether you're actually dating that person or just admiring from a distance, it is a kind of love. I remember thinking how unfair it was to hang out with him, know-ing I couldn't have him. I remember crying all night listening to "The Chain" by Ingrid Michaelson and flipping through pictures of him on Facebook at Amber's birthday party. It was HELL. DON'T DO THAT YOURSELF.

REREAD "CHAPTER 1: REASONS TO NOT STALK YOUR EX" IF YOU DOUBT ME FOR EVEN A MINUTE.

After Dan, I literally thought I'd never love again. But that was so so so NOT true.

The love I felt for Dan was a totally different kind of love. In some ways I think love is like snowflakes—casually working in a winter/ Christmas reference HOLLA—each one is different and each one FEELS different when it falls on you. But every snowflake—no matter how fast it falls or where it lands or how it tastes on your tongue—is still a snowflake, just like every love—no matter who it's with or if it's unrequited—is still love. That's why love is so exciting and impossible to resist.

With Dan it was the highest highs and the lowest lows. I loved every moment I spent with him, and hated every moment I wasn't around him. That kind of love isn't healthy.

It's one-sided and ultimately it's kind of empty. In time, that's what I learned. That kind of love doesn't work for me. Honestly, unrequited love doesn't work for anyone. It hurts. You deserve love that's returned. Everyone does.

A few years later, Dan called me out of the blue. It was the exact phone call I'd always wanted. I remember thinking, "I've waited for this day since I was fourteen years old. I prayed for this day, I wished and hoped and willed this to happen and here it is happening and . . . I don't want it."

I KNOW IT'S CRAZY, RIIIIGHT?

But it's true. I had realized I wanted a love better than that. I deserved one that wasn't just, "I'm suddenly single and lonely and drunk right now and your name is one of the first in my phone because of alphabetical order so I'm calling you because I want you to remind me how great I am." Obviously he didn't say that but I'm giving you the real-ass subtext.

I wanted someone who wanted ME for me. For who I was,not for what I did for his ego.

And you know what? I found it.

Then I lost it.

Then I found it again.

And lost it.

And found it, again.

And recently I just lost it—again.

And yes, I am heartbroken. But what my time of unrequited love taught me, what any love taught me, is that love WILL find you. It WILL come back to you. You WILL meet your someone and maybe you'll lose your someone, and you WILL survive it. All of it.

Don't settle for being the best friend.

Don't settle for less.

Be the romantic lead.

THE 16 DANGERS OF BEING IN A NON-RELATIONSHIP RELATIONSHIP

In this book, I reference what I like to call a Non-relationship Relationship, and I thought I should clarify what this is—even though I missed my deadline to write this and my editor is going to murder me. (Sorry, David. 😬.)

To get straight to it, a Non-relationship Relationship is when you are seeing someone but the other person doesn't want to "label" what the two of you together are. I have been in Non-relationship Relationships a couple times, but the last one was the most intense and, at this point, it's the last time I'm willing to do it for a while. *sigh*

This is a really tricky subject because there are a lot of people, both male and female, especially at my age, who have no problem with this kind of non-status. There are people who can successfully and happily just date someone without a commitment and be cool with it. And that's awesome. And I am super jealous of that.

But what I'm talking about is something really specific.

A couple days after I turned seventeen, I met this guy. Let's call him Greg. We became really good friends, and eventually I developed feelings for him.

It's weird cuz it wasn't that immediate, like, "Oh my god, I'm in love with him" thing.

It was a really slow progression, but I knew we were becoming more than just friends. We never even spoke about dating. I thought maybe he liked me, too, because even though we didn't see each other often, he would still try really hard to keep in touch. But at the same time, I thought maybe he just liked me as a person, which is (~weird~) possible.

I dated someone else while Greg and I were just friends, and I talked to him about those relationships, which is a very friendzoney thing to do. I told him about bad dates I'd been on and weird things guys said to me, and he always listened and made jokes and gave pretty bad advice. But still, it was appreciated. Things started to change, though, after about nine months. We started hanging out a lot more. He was someone super fun to bring to movie premieres I had to go to. Movie premieres may sound exciting—and they ARE; I mean I'm super grateful I get to make movies and go to these kinds of events—but they aren't just fun. It's kind of super stressful to go out and have a ton of photographers take your picture. It's a lot of work, and I'm not gonna lie, more people end up talking about what my shoes looked like with my dress than how the actual movie was, which is something that will hopefully change soon. Lolz

But he always somehow made it fun, and we could joke and hang during the after-parties, which really ARE fun.

Anyway, after a while I started to get super confused. Sometimes he'd act like he was my boyfriend entirely. Just giving off that VIBE, YA KNOW. It wasn't in any specific thing he did or said, but more just the way he acted toward me.

It was freaking me out, because I was starting to seriously like this guy. But we were such good friends and I didn't want to lose him as a HOMIE—but I also kinda liked him as a BOYFRIEND. We ended up having a talk, and he said he didn't want to label things. He said he did like me, but he didn't know if he was ready for a relationship but he kind of wanted to be in a relationship and could we just keep going how we were. UGH. CONFUSING. IT SUCKED. And we had the same talk a bunch of times after that. And it always ended in us arguing and me crying and drama, and then we would always end up going back to just being friends.

Now that you know MY story let's break it down:

I don't know that I'm always going to feel this way, but for now, for me, the Non-relationship Relationships do not work. I'm the first to admit that I'm a hopeless romantic. I always see things as a movie where eventually the guy will stand outside my house holding up a boom box and blasting a love song. But the reality is we don't live in the eighties and life isn't a Cameron Crowe/John Hughes movie. TRAGEDY.

Sometimes what you want isn't always what somebody else wants. I think it's really important to be fully aware of what it is you're looking for in a person and to be brutally honest about it with yourself. As much as you may think you're fine with someone not labeling your relationship, realize that kind of gives them license to go out and do whatever. And if you're fine with that, by all means go ahead. But if you're like me and you tend to realllllly fall for someone and every song you hear suddenly reminds you of them and you find yourself trying to work their name into every conversation and you wake up in the morning scared to check your phone because you don't want to feel that weird aching disappointment in your stomach if you don't see their name on your home screen and all you wonder about every day when you're walking home is "Why am I not enough for him?" . . .

Then I think you should rethink it. Everyone deserves to have someone who wants to be with them, just them. We all deserve someone who's proud to call you a boyfriend or girlfriend. And if you don't want that, that's cool. But if you do, be honest about it. Life is too short to be anxious about your relationship status. Relationships should be fun and comforting, not confusing and terrifying.

As for me, right now, I am just trying to maintain a healthy relationship with my cat, Gizmo, who is currently, definitely, emotionally manipulating me. Some days you cuddle me, Gizmo! Some days you scratch me! What do you want from me!

Why am I single?!?!

Okay . . . Well . . . Maybe I know why.

2 A.M.
(A She Poem)

He loved her when he needed to love her
When the spaces between his fingers grew lonely
And his lips too cold at night
When the space in his bed was free of visitors
And her phone was still on
When 2 A.M. drew near and the fear of waking up
alone startled him
He loved her out of fear
The terrifying prospect that the others who
amused him
Would have others who amused them
The thought that she would be the only one there
when his charm couldn't get him by
Because she was
Because she loved him
All the time
Because the spaces between her fingers were
always lonely

But they only longed for his touch
Like a puzzle
Every other set of fingers before him
Fit like the wrong key in the right door
Because the space in her bed was reserved
Only for the shape of his body
Next to hers
Because when 2 A.M. drew near
She turned off her phone
Because the fear of not hearing it ring startled her

She loved him because she needed him
He loved her
When he needed to

And the difference startled her

17

LET'S MAKE A NEW BEGINNING

There's a quote from a Semisonic song that has always meant a great deal to me. It's from the song "Closing Time," which is VERY important and nostalgic to me. It came out when I was only two, but it's been on so many sound tracks to so many rom-coms and I used to be super into the nineties and all emo so . . . ya. Anyway, one of the lyrics is about how every new beginning means something else has to come to an end.

{ That's something that has always stuck in my mind. }

I am a hopeless romantic. I choose to see the good in people. I love the idea of love and of being in a relationship. I love the comfort of having someone there all the time. I am a masochist when it comes to nostalgia. You know that feeling you get when you hear a song that reminds you so perfectly of a certain time in your life? The kind of song that whenever it's on it brings back so many waves of memories that it almost makes you nauseous? Racing through your mind, suddenly, are all these images of you and the people who once upon a time meant everything to you. I listen to those songs on repeat cuz . . . Well, IDK why . . . I guess I just ENJOY making myself miserable.

For me, another song that trips the synapses is "Texas" by Magic Man, which I was actually in the music video for—though that's not why I love it. (I fell in love with it first and tweeted about it so incessantly that the lead singer DM'ed me on Twitter to ask if I'd want to be in the video. And obviously I was like, "OH MY GOD! YESSSSSS!") I can listen to "Texas" and the happy memories just start to stir. I can remember the times we had—Summer, Joel, Adam, and I—and think, "Wow, we were such idiots" in the best way possible. Then there are other songs that bring back this weird-messed-up-shaky-nauseous-all-consuming-sadness-cut-with-the strangest-happiness-I've-ever-felt feeling.

It's this feeling that this song reminds me of the happiest time in my life—and now that time is over. And I miss it—all I can think about whilst listening to those songs is how much I miss that happiness. It's songs like "Oblivion" by Grimes and "See You Soon" by Coldplay. Also "When I'm With You" by Best Coast—but Bethany from that band is HELLA dope, so I still listen to her music ALL the time (except for said super-sad song that makes me ugly cry in bed at four in the morning). Every time I hear those songs start to come on I skip through them. Even just the opening chords can send me into a downward spiral. Which reminds me of a quote by Dante, "There is no greater sadness than to recall in misery the time we were happy."

That's not to say I haven't been happy since my time in London. I have. I am happy right now. But it's a different happiness. Because I still crave this thing I cannot have.

I miss that time in my life. I miss the beginning of 2014. I miss who I was before everything that happened. (Ignorance is bliss, right?) Sometimes I get so sad about how different I am now. I used to only believe there was good in the world. I still do see life that way. I still believe . . . But I also see it differently.

I also know that I romanticize the past, and I know that it wasn't as good as I remember it.

I also know I fall too hard for people and think they are the ONLY people in the world I could ever love. I still feel that way sometimes.

But I would rather be that way. **I would rather feel everything TOO intensely than to not feel anything at all.** I'd rather be a hopeless romantic and get hurt a million times, pick up the pieces, rearrange them, only to have someone break me again rather than believe there's nothing romantic about the world.

There is so much romance in life that has nothing at all to do with ~romance~. Let me explain.

I have fallen in love with strangers in coffee shops. I've fallen in love with the stories I read behind their eyes. I've fallen in love with couples I've seen on the streets of New York City. The way they fight on the corner of Park Avenue, screaming at one another in the cold December air before succumbing to the warmth of one another's arms. I've fallen in love with Christmas and Thanksgiving and Halloween and New Year's and the traditions they hold. The familiarity of celebrating the same thing the same way every year. I am in love with the cappuccino from a restaurant called Supper on the Lower East Side. I fall in love with songs all the time—"Holocene" by Bon Iver being maybe the first love of my life.

I've fallen in love with New York City eight hundred times over. I can't describe how much love I have for my hometown. When

I'm away sometimes, I think about New York. I imagine myself back home. I travel down her avenues, down her crooked downtown streets. I miss New York with my whole body when I'm away from her. Nowhere else in the world can I roam freely knowing eventually, no matter where I get lost, I'll find myself again. At the edge of Harlem or over by the concrete dividers on the West Side Highway. Madison Avenue or Union Square. Central Park or the center of SoHo. I can get home. I AM home. I can be wherever I want, whenever I want. And that's the closest thing I'll ever get to time traveling, I think. I feel so blessed to have been able to grow up and fall in love in my town, in my city, in New York.

I've fallen in love with my friends. I have fallen in love with nights on Lily and Raya's living room floor. Sweatpants on, my hair in a bun, no makeup, hot tea, gossip, advice, stories, anecdotes, and happiness, and hours of Cards Against Humanity. Lily, Raya, Denise, Kaleigh, and Jenni . . . **I LOVE YOU.**

The point is, love is so much more than just dating. Yes, I still believe in "The One" and I still hope to meet him. I hope to meet MANY loves of my life. I mean I'm nineteen so no need to settle down, even if right now I'm sitting in a robe drinking an espresso and reading a *Gluten-Free Living* magazine. I'm actually fifty-three. Jsyk.

Jk.

Maybe.

I hope to fall in love a million times. I think love is so wonderful and gorgeous and exciting. I want to meet many people who excite me, entice me, and make me fall for them.

After all, the fall is the best part.

The reason I wrote this chapter is because I recently have gone through a breakup. It is so hard and awful; endings are not my forte.

But it's made me realize as much as I hate endings I love beginnings. I love first hellos and the idea of starting over. And EVERY SINGLE DAY is an opportunity to start over. I believe in fate and that everything happens for a reason. So if something has just ended in your life, know it's because it was MEANT to end. It ended so that something better could take its place in your life. That has always proven to be true for me. It's that thought that guides me through the hard times. And I hope if something is ending in your life, you are able to realize that, yeah . . . That SUCKS. I miss THAT. THAT was supposed to be mine forever. It's not always FAIR. BUT . . . Know that your loss is making room for something else. No matter how much it might hurt right now.

Every new beginning means something else has to end.

So, c'mon.

Let's mak n begin

<3